A VISUAL HISTORY OF COSTUME The Sixteenth Century

JANE ASHELFORD

B T BATSFORD LTD, LONDON
DRAMA BOOK PUBLISHERS, NEW YORK

Acknowledgments

Published in Great Britain by
B. T. Batsford Ltd
4 Fitzhardinge Street
London W1H 0AH

ISBN 0 7134 4099 6

Published in USA by
Drama Book Publishers
821 Broadway
New York, New York 10003

ISBN 0 89676 076 6

Typeset by Tek-Art Ltd Kent
and printed in Great Britain by
R J Acford
Chichester, Sussex

This book could not have been written without the co-
operation of all the museums and art galleries who, in
many cases, took great trouble to provide photographs
and information about works of art in their collections.
The names of individual curators are too numerous to
list here, and I hope they will take my thanks as read.

My thanks are due to Timothy Auger and Heather
Jones of Batsford for their help in the editing of this
book.

Acknowledgement relating to the use of individual
illustrations is made in detail in the List of Illustrations.

Contents

Preface

A *Visual History of Costume* is a series devised for those who need reliable, easy-to-use reference material on the history of dress.

The central part of each book is a series of illustrations, in black-and-white and colour, taken from the time of the dress itself. They include oil paintings, engravings, woodcuts and line drawings. By the use of such material, the reader is given a clear idea of what was worn and how, without the distortions and loss of detail which modern drawings can occasionally entail.

Each picture is captioned in a consistent way, under the headings, where appropriate, 'Head', 'Body' and 'Accessories'; the clothes are not just described, but their significance explained. The reader will want to know whether a certain style was fashionable or unfashionable at a certain time, usual or unusual – such information is clearly and consistently laid out. The illustrations are arranged in date order, and the colour illustrations are numbered in sequence with the black-and-white, so that the processes of change can be clearly followed.

The pictures will be all the better appreciated if the reader has at least some basic overall impression of the broad developments in dress in the period concerned, and the Introduction is intended to provide this.

Technical terms have been kept to a reasonable minimum. Many readers will use these books for reference, rather than read them straight through from beginning to end. To explain every term every time it is used would have been hopelessly repetitive, and so a Glossary has been provided. Since the basic items of dress recur throughout the book, a conventional, full Index would have been equally repetitive; therefore the Glossary has been designed also to act as an Index; after each entry the reader will find the numbers of those illustrations which show important examples of the item concerned.

List of Illustrations

Note The subject is followed by the artist, where known (attr.= attributed), then the medium, and collection. An asterisk * indicates a colour illustration, between pages 72 and 73.

20*Jane Seymour
Hans Holbein
Oil on panel
Kunsthistorisches Museum, Vienna

21 Thomas Boleyn, 1st Earl of Wiltshire
and Ormonde (?)
Hans Holbein
Drawing
Royal Library, Windsor Castle; reproduced by
gracious permission of Her Majesty the Queen

22 Thomas, 2nd Baron Vaux
Hans Holbein
Drawing
Royal Library, Windsor Castle; reproduced by
gracious permission of Her Majesty the Queen

23 Anne Boleyn
Unknown artist
Oil on panel
National Portrait Gallery, London

24 An unknown lady
Hans Holbein
Drawing
Royal Library, Windsor Castle; reproduced by
gracious permission of Her Majesty the Queen

25 Henry VIII and his jester Will Somers
Manuscript illumination
Royal 2 A XVI f.63v.
Courtesy Trustees of the British Museum

26 Unknown man
Hans Holbein
Drawing
Courtesy Trustees of the British Museum

27 Sir John Godsalve
Hans Holbein
Drawing
Royal Library, Windsor Castle; reproduced by
gracious permission of Her Majesty the Queen

28 Thomas Howard, 3rd Duke of Norfolk
Hans Holbein
Oil on panel
Reproduced by gracious permission of
Her Majesty the Queen

29 An Englishwoman walking
Hans Holbein
Drawing
Ashmolean Museum, Oxford

30 William Parr, Marquess of Northampton
Hans Holbein
Drawing
Royal Library, Windsor Castle; reproduced by
gracious permission of Her Majesty the Queen

31 Simon George
Hans Holbein
Oil on panel
Städelsches Kunstinstitut, Frankfurt am Main

32 Mary Zouch
Hans Holbein
Drawing
Royal Library, Windsor Castle; reproduced by
gracious permission of Her Majesty the Queen

33 Mrs Pemberton
Hans Holbein
Miniature
Victoria and Albert Museum, London

34 Catherine Howard (?)
After Holbein
Oil on panel
National Portrait Gallery, London

35 Henry VIII
Unknown artist
Oil on panel
National Portrait Gallery, London

36 Lady of the Bodenham(?) family
Unknown artist
Oil on panel
The collection at Parham Park, West Sussex

37 Mary I
Master John
Oil on panel
National Portrait Gallery, London

38 Elizabeth Cobham
Brass rubbing
Victoria and Albert Museum, London

39 Lady Jane Dudley
Master John, attr.
Oil on panel
National Portrait Gallery, London

40 Edward VI
Studio of Scrots
Oil on panel
National Portrait Gallery, London

41*Edward VI
Unknown artist
Oil on panel
Reproduced by gracious permission of
Her Majesty the Queen

42 Catherine Parr
Unknown artist
Oil on panel
National Portrait Gallery, London

43 **Princess Elizabeth**
William Scrots, attr.
Oil on panel
Reproduced by gracious permission of
Her Majesty the Queen

44 **Unknown boy**
Florentine school
Oil on panel
National Gallery, London

45 **Unknown man**
Unknown artist
Oil on panel
Reproduced by gracious permission of
Her Majesty the Queen

46 **Thomas Wentworth, 1st Baron**
John Bettes, attr.
Oil on panel
National Portrait Gallery, London

47 **The Earl of Surrey**
William Scrots
Oil on canvas
National Portrait Gallery, London

48 **Eleonora of Toledo**
Agnolo Bronzino
Oil on panel
Wallace Collection, London

49 **Mary I**
Hans Eworth
Oil on panel
Fitzwilliam Museum, Cambridge

50 **Lady Jane Dudley (?)**
Unknown artist
Oil on panel
National Portrait Gallery, London

51 **Henry, Lord Maltravers**
After Eworth
Oil on panel
By kind permission of His Grace the Duke of
Norfolk

52 **Mary Neville, Lady Dacre**
Hans Eworth
Oil on panel
National Gallery of Canada, Ottawa

53 **Jane Ingleton**
Brass rubbing
Victoria and Albert Museum, London

54 **Sir John Gage and wife**
Sculpture
Firle Church; by kind permission
of Viscount Gage

55 **Unknown lady**
Hans Eworth
Oil on panel
Tate Gallery, London

56 **Queen Mary and Philip II**
Unknown artist
Oil on panel
National Maritime Museum, Greenwich, London

57 **Lady Jane Dorner**
Antonio Mor
Oil on panel
The Prado, Madrid

58 **Unknown lady**
Hans Eworth
Oil on panel
Private collection

59 **Mary, Queen of Scots**
School of Clouet
Oil on panel
Victoria and Albert Museum, London

60 **William Bullein**
Woodcut
'Bullein's Bulwarke of defence againste all
sickness' courtesy Trustees of the British Museum

61 **'Twenty-two godly and faythfull Christians'**
Woodcut
Acts and Monuments of the Martyrs. John Fox.
Courtesy Trustees of the British Museum

62 **Sir Nicholas Throckmorton**
Unknown artist
Oil on panel
National Portrait Gallery, London

63 **Henry Stuart, Lord Darnley and Charles
Stuart, Earl of Lennox**
Hans Eworth
Oil on panel
Reproduced by gracious permission of
Her Majesty the Queen

64 **Elizabeth Roydon, Lady Golding**
Hans Eworth
Oil on panel
Tate Gallery, London

65 **Theophila, wife of 3rd Earl of Worcester**
Unknown artist
Oil on panel
The Duke of Badminton

66 **Anne Browne, Lady Petre**
Steven van der Meulen, attr.
Oil on panel
The Lord Petre

67 **Mary Hilly Mrs Mackwilliam**
Master of the Countess of Warwick, attr.
Oil on panel
The Lord Tollemache

68 **Edward Windsor, 3rd Baron Windsor**
Antonio Mor
Oil on panel
The Earl of Plymouth

69 **Thomas, 2nd Baron Wentworth**
Steven van der Meulen, attr.
Oil on panel
National Portrait Gallery, London

70 **Sir Henry Lee**
Antonio Mor
Oil on panel
National Portrait Gallery, London

71 **Anthony Browne, Viscount Montague**
Hans Eworth
Oil on panel
National Portrait Gallery, London

72 **Countess of Warwick**
The Master of the Countess of Warwick, attr.
Oil on panel
By kind permission of the Marquess of Tavistock
and the Trustees of the Bedford Estates

73 **Elizabeth I and the Three Goddesses**
Monogrammist HE
Oil on panel
Reproduced by gracious permission of
Her Majesty the Queen

74***Unknown girl**
Master of the Countess of Warwick, attr.
Oil on panel
The Tate Gallery, London

75 **A Workman**
Woodcut
'A Christall Glass of Christian Reformation',
Stephen Bateman. Courtesy Trustees of the
British Museum

76 **Rich man and beggar**
Woodcut
'A Christall Glass of Christian Reformation',
Stephen Bateman. Courtesy Trustees of the
British Museum

77 **A group of English women**
Lucas de Heere
Watercolour
Add. Ms, 28330, f.33; courtesy Trustees of the
British Museum

78 **Unknown man**
Nicholas Hilliard
Miniature
Victoria and Albert Museum, London

79 **Sir Thomas Coningsby**
George Gower, attr.
Oil on panel
National Portrait Gallery, London

80 **Lady Kytson**
George Gower
Oil on panel
Tate Gallery, London

81 **Elizabeth Littleton, Lady Willoughby**
George Gower, attr.
Oil on canvas
The Lord Middleton

82 **London women and a water-carrier**
J. Hoefnagel
Engraving
Detail from 'Civitates Orbis Terrarum'

83 **James VI**
Rowland Lockey, attr.
Oil on canvas
National Portrait Gallery, London

84 **Queen Elizabeth**
Unknown artist
Oil on panel
National Portrait Gallery, London

85 **Queen Elizabeth**
Nicholas Hilliard, attr.
Oil on panel
National Portrait Gallery, London

86 **Robert Dudley, 1st Earl of Leicester**
Unknown artist
Oil on panel
National Portrait Gallery, London

87 **The Queen out hunting**
Engraving
'The noble arte of Venerie or Hunting',
G. Turbervile. Courtesy Trustees of
the British Museum

88 **The Keeper of Hounds**
Engraving
'The noble arte of Venerie or Hunting',
G. Turbervile. Courtesy Trustees of
the British Museum

89 **The Falconer**
Engraving
'The Book of Falconrie . . .', George Turbervile;
courtesy Trustees of the British Museum

90 **Three children**
Unknown artist
Oil on panel
Private Collection

91 **Robert Dudley, 1st Earl of Leicester**
Unknown artist
Oil on panel
National Portrait Gallery, London

92 **Sir Philip Sidney**
Unknown artist
Oil on canvas
National Portrait Gallery, London

93 ***Sir Martin Frobisher**
Cornelius Ketel
Oil on canvas
The Bodleian Library, Oxford

94 **Gardeners**
Woodcut
'The Gardener's Labyrinth', D. Mountain,
Courtesy Trustees of the British Museum

95 **Gardeners**
Woodcut
'The Gardener's Labyrinth', D. Mountain,
Courtesy Trustees of the British Museum

96 **Tarlton the clown**
Manuscript illumination
Harley Ms. 3885, f.19; courtesy Trustees of
the British Museum

97 **Jane Bradbuirye**
Brass rubbing
Victoria and Albert Museum, London

98 **Dame Philippa Coningsby**
English School
Oil on panel
Indianapolis Museum of Art,
James E. Roberts Fund

99 **Mary, Queen of Scots**
After portrait by Hilliard
Oil on panel
National Portrait Gallery, London

100 **Sir Nicholas Bacon**
Unknown artist
Oil on panel
National Portrait Gallery, London

101 **Sir Edward Hoby**
Unknown artist
Oil on panel
National Portrait Gallery, London

102 ***Sir Jerome Bowes**
Unknown artist
Oil on canvas
The Suffolk Collection, Ranger's House,
Blackheath, London

103 **Unknown man**
Nicholas Hilliard
Miniature
Victoria and Albert Museum, London

104 **Sir Christopher Hatton**
Possibly after Ketel
Oil on panel
National Portrait Gallery, London

105 **Elizabeth Sydenham, Lady Drake**
George Gower, attr.
Oil on canvas
Private collection

106 ***Lettice Knollys, Countess of Leicester**
Oil on canvas
George Gower, attr.
The Marquess of Bath

107 **Mary Hill, Mrs Mackwilliam (?)**
Circle of Gower
Oil on panel
The Lord Tollemache

108 **Unknown girl**
John Bettes
Oil on panel
Governers and Headmaster of St Olave's and
St Saviour's Grammar School, Orpington

109 **Unknown girl**
Detail of 108

110 **Sir Henry Unton**
Unknown artist
Oil on panel
By kind permission of His Grace the Duke of Norfolk

111 **Thomas Inwood and his three wives and
children**
Brass rubbing
Victoria and Albert Museum, London

112 **The Judgement of Solomon**
Embroidered long cushion
The National Trust, Hardwick Hall

113 **Queen Elizabeth**
Unknown artist
Oil on canvas
The Toledo Museum of Art; gift of
Edward Drummond Libbey

114 **Henry, 5th Baron Windsor**
Unknown artist
Oil on panel
The Earl of Plymouth

115 **Queen Elizabeth**
George Gower, attr.
Oil on panel
National Portrait Gallery, London

116 **Unknown man**
Nicholas Hilliard
Miniature
Victoria and Albert Museum, London

117 **Robert Sydney, 1st Earl of Leicester**
Unknown artist
Oil on canvas
National Portrait Gallery, London

118 **Mary Huddye**
Brass rubbing
Victoria and Albert Museum, London

119 ***Sir Walter Raleigh**
Attributed to 'H'
Oil on panel
National Portrait Gallery, London

120 **Giles Brydges, 3rd Lord Chandos**
Hieronimo Custodis
Oil on canvas, transferred from panel
By kind permission of the Marquess of Tavistock
and the Trustees of the Bedford Estates

121 **Francis Clinton, Lady Chandos**
Hieronimo Custodis
Oil on canvas, transferred from panel
By kind permission of the Marquess of Tavistock
and the Trustees of the Bedford Estates

122 **George Clifford, 3rd Earl of Cumberland**
Nicholas Hilliard
Miniature
National Maritime Museum, Greenwich, London

123 **Unknown girl**
Isaac Oliver
Miniature
Victoria and Albert Museum, London

124 **Sir Walter Raleigh**
Unknown artist
Oil on panel
Colonial Williamsburg photograph

125 **Part of an embroidered valance**
Victoria and Albert Museum, London

126 **Countess of Nottingham**
Marcus Gheeraerts the Younger, attr.
Oil on canvas
Viscount Cowdray

127 **Frontispiece to 'A quip for an upstart courtier'**
Woodcut
Courtesy Trustees of the British Museum

128 **Queen Elizabeth**
Marcus Gheeraerts the Younger
Oil on canvas
National Portrait Gallery, London

129 **Unknown lady**
Unknown artist
Oil on panel
Cummer Gallery of Art, Jacksonville, Florida

130 **Thomas Kennedy of Culzean**
Unknown artist
Oil on panel
In the collection of the National Trust for Scotland

131 **Thomas Blunt**
Unknown artist
Oil on panel
J. Eyston, Mapledurham House

132 **Venetian courtesan**
Engraving
'Diversarum Nationum Habitus', Pietro Bertelli, Victoria and Albert Museum, London

133 **Henry Wriothesley, 3rd Earl of Southampton**
Nicholas Hilliard
Miniature
Fitzwilliam Museum, Cambridge

134 **Sir Henry Slingsby**
Nicholas Hilliard
Miniature
Fitzwilliam Museum, Cambridge

135 **A Spanish gentleman**
Woodcut
'Des habits . . . du monde' J. de Glen
Courtesy Trustees of the British Museum

136 **Unknown lady**
William Segar, attr.
Oil on panel
Private collection

137 ***Unknown lady**
William Segar, attr.
Oil on canvas
City of Kingston-upon-Hull Museums and Galleries, Fereno Art Gallery

138 **James VI**
Unknown artist
Oil on panel
Scottish National Portrait Gallery

139 **Unknown lady and two children**
Unknown artist
Oil on panel
Private collection

140 **Unknown man**
Isaac Oliver
Miniature
Reproduced by gracious permission of
Her Majesty the Queen

141 **The life of Sir Henry Unton (detail)**
Oil on panel
Unknown artist
National Portrait Gallery, London

142 **Unknown lady**
Marcus Gheeraerts the Younger, attr.
Oil on panel
Reproduced by gracious permission of
Her Majesty the Queen

143 **Elizabeth Vernon, Countess of Southampton**
Unknown artist
Oil on panel
The Duke of Buccleuch and Queensberry

144 **The life of Sir Henry Unton (detail)**
Unknown artist
Oil on panel
National Portrait Gallery, London

145 **Robert Devereaux, 2nd Earl of Essex**
After Gheeraerts
Oil on panel
National Portrait Gallery, London

146 **William Burghley, 1st Baron Cecil**
Unknown artist
Oil on panel
National Portrait Gallery, London

147 **Unknown man**
Nicholas Hilliard
Pen and watercolour over pencil
Miniature
Victoria and Albert Museum, London

148 **The Browne brothers**
Isaac Oliver
Miniature
Burghley House Preservation Trust Limited

149 **A lady of the Talbot family**
Unknown artist
Oil on panel
Fitzwilliam Museum, Cambridge

150 **Lady Elizabeth Southwell**
Marcus Gheeraerts the Younger, attr.
Oil on canvas
The Viscount Cowdray

151 **Edward Tollemache**
Unknown artist
Oil on panel
The Lord Tollemache

152 **Francis Russell, 4th Earl of Bedford**
Robert Peake the Elder, attr.
Oil on canvas
By kind permission of the Marquess of Tavistock
and the Trustees of the Bedford Estates

153 **Elizabeth, wife of 4th Earl of Worcester**
Unknown artist
Oil on panel
The Duke of Beaufort

154 **Queen Elizabeth (?)**
Unknown artist
Oil on panel
The collection at Parham Park, West Sussex

155 **Henry Wriothesley, 3rd Earl of Southampton**
Unknown artist
Oil on panel
Lady Anne Bentinck; on loan to National Portrait
Gallery, London

156 **Charles Howard, 1st Earl of Nottingham**
Unknown artist
Oil on canvas
National Portrait Gallery, London

157 **Sir Walter Raleigh and son**
Unknown artist
Oil on panel
National Portrait Gallery, London

Introduction

The period of the Renaissance was one in which an extraordinary degree of originality and creativity was evident in the devising of new styles of dress. Fashions appeared and disappeared at what seemed to contemporaries a startlingly rapid, even indecent rate. Glorification of the individual, increased wealth and the desire to impress the world with one's social status led to an unprecedented demand for luxury fabrics, trimmings, jewels and accessories. England, immune to the impact of the Renaissance during the unstable and hazardous years of the Wars of the Roses and the precarious founding of the Tudor dynasty had, with the accession of Henry VIII in 1509, a true Renaissance prince who wanted his court to rival and indeed to surpass that of Francis I of France. The dull clothes worn at his father's court were replaced with magnificent garments fashioned from richly coloured and patterned textiles imported from Europe, their surfaces further enriched with jewels of the finest Renaissance workmanship. Set against pale lynx fur and deep brown sable were ruffles of white lawn at neck and wrist, their edges embroidered with intricate patterns of embroidery.

Court fashions, though intentionally chauvinistic, would happily incorporate any foreign style that was deemed attractive. This was a trend that reached its peak during the reign of Queen Elizabeth I when those who could afford it insisted on wearing fashions that were 'farre fetched and deere bought', producing a spate of satirical invective against the foolish Englishman who indiscriminately mixed together outrageous foreign fashions.

The England of Elizabeth was a prosperous and peaceful country and foreigners were impressed by the number of well-dressed people whom they saw in the streets. A German visitor to London in 1592 observed that acquiring fine clothes appeared to be more important to some women than having food in the house: 'The women . . . go dressed out in exceedingly fine clothes, and give all their attention to their ruffs and stuffs, to such a degree indeed, that, as I am informed, many a one does not hesitate to wear velvet in the streets, which is common with them, whilst at home perhaps they have not a piece of dry bread'. Increased expenditure on dress was not limited solely to the rich and those at court; a higher standard of living and an influx of imported goods meant that all classes in society wanted to purchase more clothes than their forefathers. William Harrison in his *Description of England* felt that this attitude was having a detrimental effect on the country's spiritual values: 'Oh, how much cost is bestowed nowadays upon our bodies and how little upon our souls! How many suits of apparel hath the one, and how little furniture hath the other! How long time is asked in decking up of the first, and how little space left wherein to feed the latter!' Harrison and other writers complained about the amount of money wasted by the aristocracy on clothing when, in his view, it should have been invested in their estates. An estimation of the cost which could be entailed when a new suit of clothes was purchased is made in Ben Jonson's play *Every Man out of his Humour* (1599): 'to be an accomplished gentleman, that is a gentleman of the time; you must give over housekeeping in the country and live altogether in the city among the gallants; where at your first appearance 'twere good you turned four or five hundred acres of your land into three or four trunks of apparel'. (Act 1, Scene 1).

Laurence Stone's paper 'The anatomy of the Elizabethan aristocracy' examined the huge debts accumulated by the aristocracy in the last years of Elizabeth's reign and concluded that one of the essential components of this display of 'conspicuous consumption' was an extravagance in dress. He cites as examples the Earl of Arundel, who owed £1023 to 42 mercers, silkmen, tailors, embroiderers and other tradesmen; the Earl of Essex owed a draper £736; and the Earl of Leicester, who was in debt to the tune of £543 for seven doublets and two cloaks. Queen Elizabeth expected her courtiers to reflect her own splendid appearance at court and she would chastise any who appeared at court in unfashionable or unflattering clothes. This engendered an atmosphere of sartorial rivalry as the courtiers tried to outshine each other and be the first to wear the latest fashion.

As male and female dress became more complex and the desire for novelty and greater ornamentation increased, specialist fashion services developed in London. The Royal Exchange, the prestigious building built by Sir Thomas Gresham and opened by Queen Elizabeth in 1571, became a by-word in contemporary literature as a treasure house of desirable goods and the meeting place for fashionable society. There one could find wig shops (the other fashionable area for wig making was Silver Street), feather shops for the elaborate and spangled hat feathers, milliners for expensive imported accessories and some ready-made garments – 'fine falling bands of the Italian cutwork', embroidered night caps, ruffs, shirts, waistcoats, perfume and gloves. The latter were a very important accessory and a wide range could be bought in London. Also in the Exchange were the stalls of starchers who stiffened linen garments, seamstresses who made linen garments, and 'drawers' who drew and devised an embroidery pattern for a garment so that the customer could then embroider it.

Fashions emanating from the court spread throughout London society (St Paul's was the place to parade in the latest fashion) and then filtered out to the country districts. The time-lag between a new court fashion and its arrival in a country area could be anything from five to fifteen years. London was the international market place for the luxury textile trade and the most exclusive mercers and jewellers were located in Cheapside, and so this was the first place to visit if the shopper's priority was to buy material for an expensive and highly fashionable outfit. Mercers specialized in costly, imported fabrics, the range of which is demonstrated by this dialogue from a French/English phrase book entitled *The Parlement of Prattlers* (1593) in which the mercer explains to his customer that he has 'good wrought velvet of Geanes [probably Genoa], sattins of Lucques [Lucca] and of Cypres [Cyprus], Chamblet without waues [unwatered], cloth of gold, cloth of siluer, damaske for damsels, Spanish taffetas, Millan [Milan] fustians, Worsteds of Norwich'. Other dialogues give a fascinating glimpse of what it was like to shop in Elizabethan London. Those who could not afford to have a new suit of clothes made could buy second-hand clothes in Birchin Lane, but to do so was a mark of social inferiority and in times of plague it could prove fatal.

Experience and knowledge of fashions in the country was shaped by visits to annual fairs and an inspection of the pedlar's wares. Shakespeare, in his portrait of Autolycus in *The Winter's Tale* gives a composite picture of the wide range of goods that these itinerant salesmen offered from lawn, trimmings and coifs to pins and perfume. Those who lived near a fairly large town were fortunate, as generally the range of materials stocked by a haberdasher was quite wide. Once the material and trimmings had been bought, they would be taken to the tailor who would charge for the labour involved and any extra materials that he had to purchase. A garment would be cut by taking a pattern from an existing one, although a letter from the son of a Shrewsbury tailor in 1594 to Sir William Langley shows the problems that this method involved: 'for the other gownes yo'r measures were so ill taken that the tailor sayes he cannot tell what to make of them.'

It is easy to imagine the excitement when a member of a country family visited London and sent his purchases back to his country home. When Philip Gawdy visited London in 1587 his sister Anne had briefed him to send her the fullest possible account of what the ladies at court were wearing and instructed him to search out the best fabric to send back to her. On reading his letters to her, one sympathizes with his bewilderment as he tries to work out which fashion he should describe to his sister: 'I fynd nothing more certayne than their uncertaynty'.

The 'new golden land' of North and South America with their extraordinary riches, strange inhabitants and customs fascinated sixteenth-century English people and frequent attempts were made to explore and colonize parts of both continents. The expansion of trade led Englishmen to sail all over the known world and to bring back goods from far-flung and exotic places. This 'hardy enterprise' meant that by the end of the century a large range of imported goods could be bought in London. There was an enormous interest not only in the dress of the American Indians, but also in the dress of all foreigners, and this led to a spate of illustrated books which showed in detail the costumes worn in every country of the world. Through the wide circulation of these books many people became aware for the first time of the distinctive characteristics of national costume. Travel abroad had become widespread during this period, with a tour of the European continent becoming an essential and established part of the young nobleman's education; its value was defined by Francis Bacon in his *Essay of Travel*: 'Travel in the younger sort is a part of education in the elder a part of experience'.

Imported silks and velvets were worn by the wealthy, the poor countryman homespun garments that were fairly coarse in texture. Their dress changed little during the century and their distinctive costume marked them out as easy prey for the Elizabethan con-man, the 'connie-catcher', if they ever found themselves in London. The contrast between the courtier's imported silks and his affected behaviour and the countryman's homespun clothes and sober demeanour was made by Robert Greene in his pamphlet 'A quip for an upstart courtier' (1592). He was not alone in voicing this opinion as it was generally felt that it was morally wrong to indulge in self-gratification and vanity. The government were more concerned about the economic repercussions of the wholesale import of foreign textiles and sought to protect the native cloth and wool trade. An act was passed in 1574 to check 'the superfluity of foreign wares', but it was almost entirely unsuccessful. The wearing of clothes was also regulated by means of sumptuary legislation. The population was divided into nine distinct categories with a detailed description of what each category was allowed to wear. Penalties in the form of fines were to be imposed on anyone who dressed in a manner not suited to his particular category. Although sumptuary legislation was begun in the fourteenth century, and ten proclamations were issued between 1559 and 1597, they do not appear to have been successful.

Certain professions and classes, however, were distinguishable by their dress. Doctors and other professional men, for example, wore long gowns and a coif under their ordinary headwear. Livery was a special dress, or uniform, worn by male servants belonging to a large household or by members of the City Companies. A bright blue livery was the usual colour but it could also be in grey, russet or tawny, with the badge or the cognizance of the household embroidered on the left sleeve. The association that the colour blue had with servitude ensured that gentlemen never wore it – a fact frequently alluded to in contemporary drama.

The most splendidly dressed person in the country was the monarch and the Tudors realized the political advantages that could be gained from wearing magnificent clothes and jewels. The dazzling outfits worn by Henry VIII on the Field of the Cloth of Gold and by Elizabeth when she received foreign dignitaries were not chosen solely for reasons of personal vanity but to impress foreigners with the wealth, and hence the strength, of England. The sight of the bejewelled Queen in her (to foreign eyes) bizarre and grandiose finery, surrounded by six beautiful Maids of Honour clad in shimmering white and silver, never ceased to astound them. One visitor even commented that 'It is more the have seen Elizabeth than thee have seen England'.

Elizabeth wore the fashions of other countries, not only because her taste in dress was eclectic but because it could be politically advantageous to do so. Her jewels were chosen for their symbolic message: in the portrait of her attributed to Nicholas Hilliard in plate 85 the jewel pendant at her breast depicts a phoenix arising from flames. The phoenix was a unique and fabulous bird which renewed itself by burning and arising from the ashes and for Elizabeth it was a symbol of her virginity and uniqueness. The Tudor rose, the lily and eglantine all appear in different forms in portraits and the inclusion of each would have had a particular significance for contemporaries. Elizabeth's association with the rose was obvious, for the double Tudor rose was a symbol of the union of the white rose of the House of York with the red rose of Lancaster. The lily and the eglantine were chosen because they were the flowers of purity and chastity.

The iconoclast campaigns of the Reformation caused an appalling amount of destruction to medieval church art and the professional embroider, deprived of his usual religious subjects, turned to the natural world and emblem books for motifs with which to embellish the garments and furnishings of his clients. The secularization of church property meant that the rich religious vestments, once the prized possessions of churches and monasteries, were converted into fashionable garments. Bess of Hardwick and Mary, Queen of Scots re-used church vestments for lay use. The embroiderer, whether professional or amateur, had a keen eye for the shape and the colour of flowers, plant, animals and insects, reproducing them with a freshness and accuracy that impressed contemporaries:

> . . . with her neeld composes
> Nature's own shape of bud, bird, branch or berry
> That even her art sisters the natural roses:
> Her inkle, silk, twin with the rubied cherry.
> Shakespeare *Pericles* Act V, Chorus.

Many of these domestic pieces of embroidery have survived and on some examples in the Victoria and Albert Museum in London tiny spangles still glitter among the faded silks. The more elaborate embroideries

that incorporated pearls and precious stones have disappeared as they would have been cut-up and re-used.

Embroidery, like poetry, could 'teach and delight' and the inclusion of emblems or other allegorical figures and conceits into the design, whether it be for a skirt or a jacket, could then be 'read' for its meaning. It was a common practice for lovers to exchange handkerchiefs and these would often be embroidered with an emblematic design which would convey a message to the recipient. Hence the meaning of a phrase in the play *Philaster* 'printing my thoughts in lawn' (Act V, Scene 1, Line 557).

After the monarch the most fashionable people in the land were the aristocracy. At Henry VIII's court, many of them had acquired wealth through the confiscation of church property during the Reformation and so wanted their dress to project an image of strength and power. As with the King's dress an artificial burliness and virility was achieved in men's dress by massive padding across the shoulders and chest and a prominently displayed cod-piece. Men wore their clothes with a swaggering bravado whereas women, whose role at court was a subservient and static one, appeared immobile in their rigid bodices and full, sweeping skirts. The brief reign of Edward VI did little to change the status quo and the main development during Queen Mary's reign was the assimilation of various features of Spanish fashion into male and female dress.

Under Queen Elizabeth's influence men's dress lost the assertive shape it had acquired during her father's reign becoming more dandified and romantic and evolving finally into the self-conscious elegance epitomized by the young man in Hilliard's miniature of 1588. Both male and female dress in the Elizabethan period were subject to the same areas of exaggeration, namely the neck, arms and hips. The contrast between the style worn at Henry's court and that worn at Elizabeth's is very marked, but it is a difference in taste rather than any fundamental change in the structure of dress. During Henry's reign men wore a series of contrasting layers, each layer cut to display a different coloured lining or the garment underneath. Panels of interlaced braid, often set with jewels, decorated the surface and frills round neck and wrist were enlivened with geometric patterns of embroidery. The chest and shoulder padding gave the wearer a rather top-heavy appearance.

Male dress in the sixteenth century consisted of five basic items – shirt, doublet, jerkin, hose and gown. The shirt, made of linen, was nearly always visible above the doublet collar and at first was gathered into a low-necked band. By 1525 it was cut higher and given a band round the neck; by 1530 this had evolved into a standing collar edged with a frill. This frill eventually developed into a ruff and so became a separate article. With the introduction of starch in the 1560s and the use of setting sticks, the ruff began to assume gargantuan proportions in a variety of styles. The shape was achieved by placing the starched, damp linen over heated sticks and then leaving it to dry. The doublet was a close-fitting garment shaped to the waist which, was fairly high until 1540. After that time the waistline was at a normal level but than gradually extended into an exaggerated point that reached well below the natural waistline. The type of doublet favoured by Henry VIII and his courtiers fitted round the neck and was fastened down the front with either hooks and eyes or ties. The skirts were long, reaching to the knee or just below. After 1540 the doublet was cut with a standing collar and this increased in height until it reached its maximum at the end of the 1560s. Henry's doublets were made from the richest fabrics and included silver brocades, taffeta, satin and velvet and he wore them with hose of a contrasting colour. To create a decorative pattern the surface of the doublet was slashed and the puffs of the shirt underneath pulled through. The doublet could also be pinked, embroidered and trimmed with lace and braid. Sleeves were also subject to a variety of shapes; they could have a puffed-out fullness at the shoulder or be full and paned from shoulder to wrist or be cut wide so that they sloped to a close fit round the wrist. A hanging sleeve of a different colour and material could be worn with the wearing sleeve. Detachable sleeves were joined to the armhole of the doublet by points (ties tipped with metal tags) and it was fashionable from the late 1540s onwards to hide this join with a wing. The wing then became an ornamental feature and was treated in a number of ways. Along the lower border of the doublet were pairs of eyelet holes corresponding with similar pairs along the waistline of the hose. Points were threaded through the opposite holes and knotted in a series of bows round the waist uniting the legwear and the doublet. The ties could either be displayed as a decorative feature or concealed. The possibilities in the design of doublets were so great that a contemporary commented that a young man who wished to be thought fashionable might well need to 'lie ten nights awake, carving the fashion of a new doublet'.

Over the doublet could be worn a jerkin, a sleeved or sleeveless garment whose shape was dictated by the style of doublet underneath. The type worn by Henry VIII and his court had a wide U-opening to the waist so that the doublet could be seen. This style had become unfashionable by about 1540 and was replaced by a style that was closed down the front and had a low stand-up collar. Over doublet and jacket was worn a broad-shouldered and loose gown with ample folds falling to mid-knee or just below, from a fitting yoke. The gown, usually fur-lined, was made open down the front and the edges had turned-back border which broadened out over the shoulders. Sleeves could be puffed-out on the shoulder, to be gathered into a band at elbow level, with the rest of the sleeve left as a hanging sleeve; or they could be cut into a long, tubular shape with a horizontal or vertical slit for the arm, the rest of the sleeve left to fall as a hanging sleeve. The cloak, a fashion introduced from the European continent in the mid-1540s soon ousted the gown and it became, in its ankle-length form, the dress of the professional classes, although fur-lined

loose gowns were worn at home for warmth.

The hose consisted of two parts: upper or trunk hose, also known as breeches and lower or nether hose which could either be canions or stockings. The term hose can refer to either part as it was not used to refer solely to stockings until the middle of the seventeenth century. Before 1570 the upper hose and stockings were usually sewn together to form a single garment but after that date they were increasingly worn as separate articles, united by garters or points. The most popular form of upper hose was, by 1558, the trunk hose, variously called trunk slops, trunk breeches, round hose or French hose, its increasingly swollen shape achieved by means of padding and stiffening with several linings. A very early form of trunk hose is worn by the Earl of Surrey in a portrait attributed to William Scrots. Unlike the later form in which the fullness begins at the waist, Surrey's is distended from the fork to mid-thigh. The cod-piece was worn with hose until the middle of the 1570s and its prominent shape was accentuated by padding.

During the reign of Henry VIII various European continental fashions were absorbed into English dress, head-wear being particularly receptive. The Milan bonnet had been introduced from Italy in about 1455 and appears with some frequency in expense accounts from 1511 onwards. It had a soft ample crown and broad brim turned well up and fastened at the sides with aglets, a jewel or a medallion. The French bonnet, a bonnet with a turned-up brim that hid the crown and encircled the head like a halo, was extremely popular from the 1520s to about 1550. It was worn with a pronounced sideways tilt and was decorated with ostrich feathers and, in the one worn by Simon George, small enamelled ornaments.

The visit of King Philip II of Spain to England in 1554 to marry Queen Mary ensured the predominance of Spanish fashion for many years. The features of Spanish dress that particularly appealed to the English were the cloak – a hooded hip-length cloak whose circular edge was decorated with guards of velvet or other silk, the sleeveless paned jerkin, strong vertical lines and a severe colour scheme. When the Duke of Mantua visited England in 1557 he noticed that 'The men usually wear a doublet with a long cloth gown lined with fur down to the ground. Those who wear cape and jerkin used heretofore to dress in the Italian fashion and they are now commencing that of Spain. Those who wear a Spanish cape have their sword and buckler carried by one of their servants.' Despite the war with Spain in the 1580s, a Spanish leather jerkin, usually perfumed, leather boots, gloves and hat were considered to be an essential part of the fashionable man's wardrobe.

At the accession of Queen Elizabeth I in 1558 men's dress was generally restrained and dignified with rich, dark colours set off by white ruffles at neck and wrist and enlivened by gold and blackwork embroidery, slashing and a profuse use of aglets. The clothes followed the lines of the body fairly closely and, apart from the shape of the trunk hose, there was little exaggeration of any one feature. During the 1560s and 1570s padding centred more and more on the doublet so that its belly could be extended into an artificially curved point. Sleeves were padded and trunk hose shrank in size until, in the 1580s, it was merely a narrow pad round the hips with canions – a close-fitting tube of material covering the area from the thigh to the knee. The head was either encircled by a wide ruff or framed by a falling band; the hair was worn long and arranged in curls. The resulting silhouette was a somewhat effeminate one, with the tapering torso balanced on legs clad in coloured silk stockings and a cloak thrown nonchalantly over one shoulder. In the 1590s the taut, tense lines of padded sleeve, doublet and hose gave way to a more relaxed style as the fit of the doublet became looser and it was worn undone. Wearing both shirt and doublet undone and a large-brimmed hat was a sign that the wearer was in the fashionable state of melancholy, his mind too distracted to worry about the details of his appearance. Another visual indication that a man was in love with his mistress was to wear her favours; a selection of these are listed in the play *How a man may choose a good wife from a bad* (1602) when the hero explains that he was once a melancholic person,

> . . . a busk-point wearer,
> One that did use much bracelets of haire,
> Rings on my fingers, Jewels in mine eares,
> And now and then a wenches Carkanet,
> That had two letters for her name in Pearle
> Scarves, garters, bands, wrought wastcoats.

The use of dress as a visual statement of an idea or mood is apparent in this comment by the clown to Orsino, Duke of Illyria, in Shakespeare's play *Twelfth Night*: 'Now the melancholy god protect thee: and the tailor make thy doublet of changeable taffeta, for thy mind is a very opal' (Act 11, Scene 4, Line 73).

A visitor to the English court in 1599 observed that the main influence on male fashion was French: 'the lords and esquires of the royal court were very grand, for the most part clad in French fashion, except for their short cloaks and occasional Spanish capes, while they do not wear such broad hats as the French'. When the costume of the Elizabethan gallant was criticized by his contemporaries, it was usually because he wore a disparate collection of garments culled from several countries. Three writers: Hall, Rowlands and an anonymous dramatist, were all agreed that the essential ingredients for the fashionable look was a French doublet, Spanish hat, German or Dutch hose and Italian neckwear.

It was the elaborate and frequently effeminate dress worn by a very few fashionable gentlemen that was most susceptible to criticism and many of the most affected, and consequently most reviled, fashions originated from France, in particular from the court of Henry III (1574-89) a weak, ineffectual man controlled by his powerful mother Catherine de Medici. He enjoyed the company of a band of fawning young men whom he nicknamed 'Les Mignons'. They dressed up in female attire, wore make-up, curled their hair, smothered themselves in perfume and generally extended fashion to its most bizarre limits. Some of the fashions that were copied from the French court were the use of feather fans and make-up – 'When a plum'd fan may shade thy chalked face' (1597) – single earrings and lovelocks. It was a combination that led a contemporary to write in despair that the tough Englishman of King Henry VIII's day had become 'The world's ape of fashion'.

To the foreigner the ladies at Henry's court would have seemed rather quaint and old-fashioned in their heavy, sumptuous clothes as depicted in Holbein's drawings and paintings. The unique English contribution to fashion, the gable or pediment headdress, was a cumbersome structure that contrasts with the more delicate headdresses favoured by Italian and French ladies. It was worn over a coif (a linen cap) which completely hid the hair. The Venetian ambassador to England, 1531, described its appearance: 'They wear a sort of coif of white linen, from under which a few tresses are visible over the forehead, but the coif fits close behind so that toward the ears everything is covered, the coif concealing their hair'. With the advent of the French hood in the 1530s, the hair reappears and it is worn straight and smooth from a centre parting.

The basic elements of female dress until the middle of the century were a united bodice and skirt worn under a voluminous gown. During the second half of the century bodice and skirt were made as separate garments and the gown was relegated to the status of optional overgarment. The side-fastening bodice of the kirtle encased the upper half of the body in a rigid shape that ended, until about 1540, in a rounded waistline. The square, slightly curved neckline was cut very narrow and tight on the shoulder and it must have made any movement of the arms extremely difficult as they would have been weighed down by the massive oversleeve with turned-back cuff and the stiff, often quilted, undersleeve. This type of bodice was worn with a gored skirt that expanded from the waistline without folds, presenting a smooth, unbroken surface which could have an inverted-shaped opening so that the decorative underskirt could be displayed. A Spanish device, called the farthingale, which consisted of a series of hoops that increased in circumference from waist to feet giving the skirt placed over it a pronounced bell-like shape, appeared first in Royal Wardrobe Accounts of 1545, the fashion soon spreading to the nobility and within a decade or so it was worn by ladies of all classes, eventually being superseded in the 1590s by the French farthingale which gave the skirt a more bizarre, wheel shape.

In women's dress the ruff, that distinctive feature of Elizabethan costume, had its origins in a small strip or band of fine linen attached to the top of the chemise; the fabric was gathered so that it formed a frill, the edge of which was often embroidered. By 1559 the closely pleated and decorated layers rose up at the sides to frame the lady's face and, as with the men's dress, in the next decade it had become a separate accessory increasing gradually in size until it was wide enough to accommodate flowers and jewels in the pleats. Variations like the open fan-shaped ruff soon followed.

In the first forty years of the sixteenth century a gown was worn over the kirtle. The gown was a garment with a square neckline that fitted to the waist to fall to the ground in voluminous folds so masking the kirtle underneath. In about 1545, when the bodice and skirt were made as separate items, and the term kirtle applied to the skirt alone, the gown could not have such a prominent position and it consequently changed in style. Two styles, the loose and the close-bodied appear in portraits of the 1550s the later style was worn by Queen Mary. The Venetian ambassador, Giacomo Soranzo, wrote in 1554 that Queen Mary wore a 'gown such as men wear, but fitting very close, with an under- petticoat which has a very long train; this is her ordinary costume, being also that of the gentlewomen of England'. The loose gown was also called an open gown and it fell in folds from the shoulders. The nightgown was an ankle-length version of the loose gown which could be worn indoors or outside. As it usually had a warm fur lining it could also be worn as a dressing gown when the wearer felt unwell.

When Elizabeth came to the throne in 1558 female dress had not changed substantially for thirty years and had evolved into a rather rigid and emphatic style which was severely pyramidal in shape. The symmetry and regularity of Renaissance dress was in complete contrast to the fanciful costume of the medieval period which had favoured spiky, pointed shapes, a taste which, however, was re-established with the neo-medieval cult of the 1580s and 1590s. Fashion moved at a much faster pace during the first two decades of the reign and the dignified sobriety of the 1550s was replaced with the livelier fashions of the 1560s. The surface of the gown, bodice and skirt became broken up by applied decoration; jewellery, puffs and slashes were employed to expose material of a different colour and the contrast between plain colours and the black-and-white embroidered patterns on sleeves and ruff became more marked. The brighter colours of the 1560s can best be appreciated in the portrait of an unknown girl in the Tate Gallery dated 1569 – a mixture or red, gold, black and white.

There was a proliferation of new colours during Elizabeth's reign and they were assigned 'phantastical' names such as 'gooseturd green, pease-porridge tawny, popinjay blue, lusty gallant, and the devil-in-the-head'. Each colour would be obtainable in a variety of tones, as from the palest pink of 'maiden's blush' to the vivid red of 'lustie gallant'. Colours in the 1570s were bold; Lady Kytson painted by Gower in 1573 wears a bright red gown with black fur collar and blackwork embroidered sleeves. Fashion became highly inventive during the 1570s and a wide range of styles and decoration became available.

During the latter half of the '70s the female silhouette became fuller and stiffer and in the '80s the shape that we think of as typically Elizabethan had evolved. The stiff, heavily boned bodice compressed the bust and when it was worn with a stomacher, an inverted triangle of stiffened material, allowed it to finish in an extended point that rested on the skirt. Sleeves become a focal point, as their swollen, padded surface was embellished with large-scale embroidery. The steep lines of the Spanish farthingale skirt and the narrow, elongated bodice had the effect of making the hips look slender, the enormous width of the distended skirt being balanced by the width across the shoulders. The ruff, slightly tilted, projected outwards round the neck and completely separated head from body.

In the 1590s the inverted triangle of the stiffened stomacher becomes longer and narrower and extends well into the elliptical and then rectangular shape of the wheel farthingale skirt. The shorter skirt length and higher hairstyle, aided by wired hair ornaments, gave the whole figure a rather unbalanced appearance the rendering of which was not helped by the rather shaky perspective of most full-length portraits.

The sharp, spiky shapes and cut-up surfaces encrusted with sparkling decoration that are apparent in portraits of fashionable ladies in the closing years of Elizabeth's reign contrast with the smoothly rounded lines and sober colours of the 1550s. The late Elizabethan style was one of carefully contrived fantasy and emanated from a court spiritually in tune with the romantic and picturesque features of the medieval world – a world that was re-enacted by Elizabeth's knights who jousted and tilted for her favour in elaborate fancy dress. Ladies in 'strange fantastick habit' entertained the Court by performing in masques, their costume an eclectic mixture of heavily embroidered glittering fabrics with details copied from foreign dress and with hints of classical dress as it was understood by the theatrical designers of Italy and the Low Countries.

The Elizabethan predilection for distorted shapes and an intricately patterned surface was also a characteristic of painting, architecture and the decorative arts. Whether it be the use of a strong coiling pattern in blackwork embroidery or the dramatic silhouette of Hardwick Hall emphasis was all important. Clothes were also intended to please the senses – the sense of sight by colour and pattern, the sense of touch by embellishment of the surface and the combination of different fabrics, and the sense of smell by perfume. But whatever the intention, the end result was decidedly 'strange and stately' and 'aym'd wholly at singularitie'.

PLATES & CAPTIONS

1 Henry Spelman and wife, 1496

Note When a long gown is worn with a mantle as here and in plate 7 it is probably the attire of a civic dignitary. The simple lines of the lady's substantial kirtle and ornamental belt are typical of the dress of the gentry in the reign of Henry VI.

Head The wife wears the very early form of English hood in which an arched structure without lappets frames the face. Her husband wears his hair long to the nape of the neck and a forehead fringe.

Body The rounded neckline of the lady's kirtle is filled in with folds of material; the close-fitting sleeves end in a treble cuff of fur. Her kirtle moulds itself to the upper half of her body and it then falls in voluminous folds to the ground; the hem is decorated with a deep border of fur. Her husband wears a sleeveless mantle with a narrow collar over an ankle-length gown; the bulk of the material has been thrown over the left shoulder. His gown sleeves are wide and cuffed.

Accessories The lady wears a belt with a single clasp across her hips, one long end is tipped with a metal tag. Both have a string of beads attached to their belts.

2 Elizabeth of York, 1500-3
Unknown artist

Note In this early form of English hood, also called gable or pediment head-dress, the hair, smooth from a centre parting, is visible (it was not after 1525). The gable shape was achieved by a wired or stiffened framework and would always be worn over an undercap.

Head A border of gold set with rectangular rubies frames the face. Over it peaks the black velvet English hood. Two sets of lappets, one plain, the other decorated with pearls and jewels, fall in front of the shoulders, the rest of the hood falls behind.

Body The low, square neckline of the gown is partly filled in by folds of material; fur lining edges the front opening of the gown; bands of striped and pearl-studded material border the neckline and form a central band. The fullish sleeves end in turned-back cuffs.

Accessories Pearls arranged in a square are attached to a thin black cord around the neck.

ELIZABETHA · VXOR
HENRICI · VII ·

3 Henry VII, 1505
M. Sittow

Note The arrangement of the gown sleeves can be seen more clearly in the full-length drawing by Holbein of Henry VII for the mural in Whitehall Palace. The vertical slit in the sleeve is a large oval shape cut out of the sleeve from just below the shoulder to the elbow, so disclosing the lining and undersleeve. The sleeve continues to the wrist as a full, wide shape. Henry was elected a Knight of the Order of the Golden Fleece in 1491 by Emperor Maximilian, the first of the few English kings so honoured.

Head A cap of blocked felt with the brim turned up around the crown is worn over brushed-back longish hair.

Body A brown fur tippet is worn over a gold-and-red brocade gown with split sleeves. The white fur lining of the gown is turned back to form revers. A black doublet is worn under the gown.

Accessories A collar of the Order of the Golden Fleece is worn over the tippet.

22

4 Henry VII, 1508-9
P. Torrigiano

Note The rather austere, undecorated dress worn by Henry VII was in marked contrast to that worn by his flamboyant son.

Head A cap of blocked felt with a ridge front and back and brim turned up at the back only. The hair touches the shoulder and is brushed under.

Body The standing collar of the doublet projects above the collarless gown; the sleeves are cut to show the ermine fur lining and this lining also forms revers that are crossed over in front. The heavy folds of the gown fall from the shoulder seam. Under is worn a doublet with a centre fastening.

23

5 J. Wyddowsoun, 1513

Note There is very little difference between the shape of this lady's kirtle and the earlier one in plate 1. Her simple linen hood, if worn over an understructure, could be turned into the gable head-dress.

Head A linen hood with hanging lappets frames the lady's face.

Body The kirtle bodice fits closely to the waist from where it falls in ample folds to a fur-bordered hem. A fold of material is tucked into the neckline of the bodice; the narrow sleeves end in furred cuffs.

Accessories A belt draped around the waist is worn with a double clasp; from it are suspended beads and a purse.

6 Henry VIII, c.1520
Unknown artist

Note Henry here wears the low-necked shirt and doublet which is replaced by a high-necked style in about 1525. The Venetian ambassador, who saw him in 1519, commented that when Henry heard that Francis I had grown a beard he 'allowed his own to grow, and as it was reddish, he had then got a beard that looked like gold . . . his clothes were very rich and superb'.

Head A Milan bonnet trimmed with aglets and a large jewel. The hair reaches to the nape of the neck.

Body The low oval line of the shirt, gathered into a band, leaves the neck bare. The neckline of the doublet follows that of the shirt and is slashed at regular intervals. The doublet sleeves are cut away to form narrow decorated strips and there is a narrow ruffle at the wrist. The full sleeves of the gown have horizontal bands of decoration.

Accessories A massive pearl and jewel collar is worn on the chest and an octagonal pendant is worn on a thin black cord.

7 J. Marsham and wife, 1525

Note Neither is wearing fashionable dress; it belongs to a period of some twenty years earlier, – a feature also of other brasses. It is possible that the man's combination of mantle and gown was the ceremonial dress of a mayor.

Head The lady's hood is the style transitional between that worn by Elizabeth of York (2) and the ladies of the More family (10). The decorated lappets hang short of the turned-out lappets of the undercap to which it is attached. The man's hair hangs to the nape of the neck; he has a fringe and is clean-shaven.

Body The square neckline of the lady's fur-lined gown is filled in with a buttoned partlet. She wears ornamental bands and close-fitting sleeves with fur cuffs. The gown fits to below waist level from where it falls in folds; the trained skirt has been caught up at the back and arranged so that the fur lining is visible. The small standing collar of the man's shirt is visible above the round neckline of his sleeveless mantle which is buttoned on the right shoulder. The lining is turned back over the other shoulder and allowed to fall in folds. The gown sleeves are full with wide expansion towards the wrists, where thay are turned back into pendulous fur cuffs.

Accessories The lady wears a low-slung belt with triple clasps, pomander, beads and crucifix.

8 An Italian nobleman, 1526
Moretto

Note The sleeveless jerkin and sombre colours worn by this elegant man reflects the dominance of Spanish fashion in Italy after the decisive battle of Pavia in 1525. The unusual head-wear is typically Italian and a similar arrangement can be found in Holbein's portrait of Sir Nicholas Carew, 1532-33, in Drumlanrig Castle, Scotland.

Head A red pleated bonnet with a medallion of St Christopher is worn over a gold turban-like coif. He has a beard and moustache.

Body The standing collar of the shirt is embroidered in grey and gold and a very narrow frill is attached to the top edge. A sleeveless, V-necked black jerkin is worn undone over a slashed maroon-coloured doublet. The embroidery on the shirt can be glimpsed through the slashes and the shirt sleeve is gathered into a band with a narrow frill. A black damask cloak is thrown over one shoulder. The early form of the trunk hose matches the doublet, its surface is cut up and the lining pulled through and it is finished in a band above the knee. The cod-piece and stockings match.

Accessories A sword is attached to the belt and very tight leather gloves with extended cuffs are held in the hand. The shoes are flat and black with rounded toes and a narrow strap across the instep.

M · D · X X V I ·

9 The Triumph of Maximilian I, 1526
H. Burgkmair

Note The Emperor Maximilian organized these Swiss mercenary fighters, or *Landsknechten* as they were known, into the most effective fighting force in Europe. Their unique and eccentric costume, evolved out of necessity and characterized by excessive slashing, puffing and particolour, was copied by fashionable society. The interest in surface decoration is also apparent in the armour.

Head The man in the foreground on the left wears a laurel wreath on his head and on his back, secured by cords, he wears a hat composed of two layers each divided and folded back and decorated with ostrich feathers. The other man wears his hat at an angle; the crown is encircled with a laurel wreath. A separate attachment of feathers is worn on the back.

Body Both men wear full-sleeved shirts under their jackets; the sleeves of the man on the left have been cut in a spiral of slashed strips. The other man's sleeves are divided by tight bands into a series of narrow slashed strips. Both wear jackets that fit the upper part of the body closely. One man's tight hose has been cut at irregular intervals into a series of slashed loops so that it droops over the knee where it is tied with a sash. The hose worn by the other man is slashed horizontally across trunk, thigh, knee and calf.

Accessories Both men wear sashes tied across their bodies and simple, flat shoes.

| 1 | 2 | 3 | 4 | 5 | 6 | 7 | 8 | 9 | 10 |

10 Sir Thomas More and his family, 1526
H. Holbein

Note Holbein's drawing is a unique record of
the dress worn by members of a famous and
wealthy family. There is a marked contrast
between the fashionable dress of the younger
men and the consecutive dress of the older
members. The collar of linked S's signified the
allegiance or adherence of the wearer to the
house of Tudor and so it appears in many
portraits of members of Henry VIII's court.

Head Ladies 1,2,9 and 10 (numbering from left
to right) wear a later form of the English hood in
which one or both lappets are pinned up with
crossed bands of striped material concealing the
hair. The back curtain of fabric could either be
left free (2,10) or be pinned up (1,9). The two
younger girls (4,8) wear the rounder linen head-
dress fastened under the chin. The older men
wear caps of the old-fashioned square style. The
younger man (7) wears a bonnet tilted at the
fashionable angle.

Body The ladies (except 8) wear square-necked
kirtles under their gowns; the neckline is filled in
with buttoned partlets and necklaces. Their
front-fastening gowns have heavy, slightly
trained skirts (no.2 has her gown caught up).
The deep cuffs of their sleeves have been turned
back to reveal full, quilted undersleeves cut
along the back seam to display puffs of chemise.
The short gown worn by no.6, has a standing
collar and braid-trimmed sleeves puffed to the
elbow and then cut straight. The gown worn by
no.7 has a bulky fullness gathered onto a yoke
and straight sleeves from the elbow. Sir
Thomas's father (3) wears a judge's mantle with
the bulk of the material resting over his right
arm, under it is the judge's robe. Sir Thomas
wears a gown with broad fur revers and slit
sleeves from which emerge puffed undersleeves.

Accessories The ladies wear low-slung sash-
like girdles one of which ends in tassels (1). Sir
Thomas wears a collar of linked S's and holds a
muff, as does his father.

The Lady Barkley.

11 Elizabeth Dauncey, 1526-7
H. Holbein

Note Elizabeth (no.1 in the previous drawing) was the second daughter of Sir Thomas More. Holbein shows in this drawing the complexity of headwear at this period. The extract structure and method of assemblage of it has not been determined.

Head This is the next stage in the development of the English hood. The first layer that extends to chin level is the undercap, the second is the decorated lappet turned back on itself. The gable shape that would be clearly visible from the front is emphasized by the two rolls of striped material that meet in the centre of the forehead and conceal the hair. The two sections of the back curtain of the hood (clearly visible in the drawing) have been pulled up and over to be crossed on top of the head and project slightly over it.

Body The low, square neckline of the gown is cut away in front to end in a wide V below the waist and it is laced across the kirtle bodice underneath which, Holbein notes, was red (rot). The frill attached to the chemise under the bodice can be seen and the delicate bead necklace is wound around the neck and down the partlet to disappear into the the bodice. The round neckline of the transparent linen partlet is

secured with a pearl button. There is a deep turned-back cuff on the gown sleeve on the right arm.

12 Cecily Heron, 1526-7
H. Holbein

Note Cecily (no.8 in group drawing) was the third and youngest daughter of Sir Thomas More.

Head She wears the rounder style of linen head-dress. This is set further back on the head, so displaying the centre parting of the hair and consists of a variety of layers to one of which – probably the outer – is attached a strap which passes under the chin. A veil falls behind the shoulders.

Body The frill above the square neckline of the kirtle bodice belongs to the chemise underneath; a fold of material has been tucked in on either side. The edges of the gown worn over the kirtle veer away from the top ties that connect them and it is possible that this is to accomodate Cecily's pregnant condition. The sleeves are full and voluminous.

Accessories A tiny necklace is wound around her neck to disappear into the bodice. She also wears a large oval pendant on a riband.

13 Anne Cresacre, 1526-7
H. Holbein

Note Anne (no.4 in the group drawing) was married to Sir Thomas's son John (no.6 in the group). Her dress is the most fashionable, the contrast between the rigidity of the upper half of the body and the wide expanse of the oversleeves becomes a marked characteristic of female fashion during the next two decades.

Head Anne wears the same head-dress as Cecily Heron (no.12). It consists of three, or possibly four, layers with a curtain of heavy black material hanging to just below the shoulders.

Body A round-necked, centrally fastened partlet and thin chain fill in the low square neckline. Her gown appears to be made of a patterned material and it curves across the kirtle bodice with the embroidered edge of the chemise projecting above it. The narrow sleeve of the gown is joined by a deep turned-back cuff.

Accessories A sash-like girdle is tied just below the waistline with something suspended from it.

The Lady Eliot

15 Margaret, Lady Elyot, c.1532
H. Holbein

Note The tubes of material attached to the
English hood here use less material and could be
worn loose and flowing or could be pinned up in
various ways on top of the head-dress.

Head This three-quarter view shows how
tightly the hood encased the head and hair.
Crossed bands of material hide the hair-line and
the lappet of the undercap fits closely against the
cheek with the decorated lappet of the hood
curling away from it to form a pointed shape on
the top of the head. At the back of the hood is a
box-like section to which are attached two long
flat tubes of black velvet; the seam of the left-
hand one is clearly visible. Both fall behind the
shoulders.

Body The standing collar of the chemise has
been turned back from the tie. A pendant on a
chain has been sketched in.

14 Catherine of Aragon, c.1530
Unknown artist

Note Catherine married Henry VIII in 1509 after the death of his brother
Arthur in 1502. Her taste for sombre colours, rich brocades and large-scale
jewellery was typically Spanish. She has erroneously been accredited with
the introduction into England of blackwork or 'Spanish work' as it was
once called.

Head Catherine wears the early style of English hood. A narrow band of
gold and jewels curves inwards onto the face and forms a peak above the
forehead. Under this point striped rolls of material cover the hair. Lappets
of cloth of gold brocade are taken up and pinned on top of the hood. The
rest of the black velvet hood spreads out behind the shoulders.

Body The square neckline of the tightly fitting brown bodice is edged
with pearls and jewels set in gold mounts. Above it is the delicately
embroidered frill of a chemise. Full undersleeves of gold brocade are
closed with wrist frills. The deep cuff of the gown is folded back almost to
the shoulder.

Accessories A massive cross set with emeralds and three pearl drops is
worn on a narrow gold chain which, after three twists around the neck,
disappears into the bodice.

16 An unknown English lady, c.1535
H. Holbein

Note Holbein not only meticulously delineated
the details of dress but also recorded
contemporary stance and posture. The complex
cut of the sleeves could best be appreciated
when the wearer clasped her hands together at
waist level.

Head An English hood of the later style in
which the lappets are pinned up on top and the
hair is concealed by crossed bands; a linen
undercap swerves onto the face. The back view
shows how the back of the hood has evolved into
a distinctive box-like shape to which are attached
two tubes of material.

Body The low neck of the kirtle has been cut
square in front. Across this area, and the rest of
the bodice, a profusion of chains and strings of
tiny beads have been placed. The bodice fits
closely to the upper half of the body and then
swells out in thick folds from the waistline. The
back view shows how the pleats in the V-necked
bodice lead to the fullness of the trained skirt.
The oversleeves have immense turned-back
cuffs and undersleeves that have been slashed
along the back seam so that puffs of chemise can
be pulled through.

Accessories A rope of beads is held in the
hands.

17 Margaret Pole, Countess of Salisbury, c.1535
Unknown artist

Note This portrait, Anglo-Flemish in style, was painted sometime in the
mid-1530s and repainted in the late seventeenth/early eighteenth century
when all the ermine spots, barrel jewel on the wrist, and monogram were
added.

Head This is an early version of the English hood made of ermine and
worn without an ornamental border.

Body The low-cut bodice of dark grey is edged with ermine and the
embroidered frill of a chemise. A tiny bead necklace has been wound twice
around the neck to disappear into the bodice. The ermine cuffs of the
bodice are worn over grey quilted undersleeves cut to show puffs of
chemise. A kerchief has been draped over both shoulders.

Accessories A gold jewel shaped like a barrel on a black ribbon is worn
round the wrist of the right hand; a coral bracelet is also worn. A 'W'
monogram is held in the fingers of the right hand. Narrow rings are worn
on both hands.

33

18 Henry VIII, 1536
Joos van Cleve (attr.)

Note Henry's love of jewels and desire for flamboyant display increases as he rapidly puts on weight until the massive surface area of his dress is broken up with slashing and encrusted with applied decoration.

Head Over his short, shaved hair he wears a black velvet bonnet. The underside of the brim is decorated with pearls, jewel-spangled ostrich plume and a coloured enamel medallion of the Virgin Mary.

Body The shirt is gathered into a narrow neckband of gold set with pearls and jewels – a decoration that is continued down the front opening of the shirt. A small frill is attached to the neckband. The neckline of the gold brocade doublet has been cut straight across; lozenge-shaped slashes filled with puffs of the shirt underneath are framed by jewelled bands with large pearl ornaments and knots at the intersections. The doublet's matching sleeves have been decorated in a similar way. The gown has a wide sable collar that spreads across the shoulders and its sleeves are embroidered with seed pearls.

34

19 Henry VIII, 1536
After H. Holbein

Note Male dress was intended to enhance and exaggerate the wearer's masculinity and this was achieved by creating a massive chest and wide shoulder. Henry adopts the aggressive and dominant stance that was an essential part of this image.

Head The halo brim of the bonnet is decorated with jewels and trimmed with an ostrich feather and worn at an angle.

Body The narrow frill of the shirt is turned down over the small standing collar of the doublet. The gold brocade doublet is slashed at regular intervals to disclose puffs of the shirt underneath; the puffs are caught with square-cut jewels. The matching sleeves of the doublet are decorated in a similar way and finished with a wrist frill. Over the doublet is worn a jerkin with a wide U-opening to the waist; its full deep skirts hide the hose. A prominent cod-piece has been decorated so that it matches the doublet. The top garment is a short gown that is bordered and lined with fur. The extremely broad shoulders of this garment have a puffed-out upper section that ends above the elbow, allowing the rest of the sleeve to continue as a hanging section. Bands of interlaced cord decoration on the gown sleeve are repeated as a border on the hem.

Accessories A sash has been tied around the waist, and a second sash lower down has a dagger attached to it. A pearl-studded collar is worn across the chest and under it hangs a large gold medallion. A garter of the Order of the Garter is worn round the right knee. The King's shoes have square toes and slashed uppers.

20 Jane Seymour, 1536
H. Holbein

See colour plate between pp. 72 and 73.

21 Thomas Boleyn, 1st Earl of Wiltshire and Ormonde (?) 1530-5
H. Holbein

Note It is thought that this is Thomas Boleyn, father of Anne (23) and brother-in-law to the Duke of Norfolk (28). The combination of jerkin and slashed central section is similar to that worn by Henry VIII (19).

Head A flat cap is worn at an angle. The hair is brushed smoothly under to the nape of the neck with a forehead fringe. He wears a moustache and a full, square beard.

Body The square neckline of the shirt leaves the neck bare. The edge of the shirt is visible above the tabbed border of a garment that could either be a doublet or a plackard (a separate accessory that covered the chest and could be very ornamental). This fills in the U-shaped opening of the jerkin, which is tied in the centre of the waistline, its skirt falling in fairly tight pleats. Over it is worn a gown with a swollen upper section that appears to be cut in panes, and a full lower sleeve.

Accessories A sash girdle is worn from which something (probably a dagger or pouch) is suspended.

22 Thomas, 2nd Baron Vaux, 1532-5
H. Holbein

Note Holbein's labelling of this drawing tells us that the gown had carmine sleeves with a front panel of slashed white velvet edged with silver, or red doublet with panels of silver, white velvet and gold.

Head A similar flat cap and hairstyle to Thomas Boleyn is worn. Vaux, however, wears his beard cut into a long, pointed shape.

Body The ties attached to the embroidered standing collar have been left undone, so revealing the V-shaped opening of the shirt. The puffed-out and slashed sleeve of the gown has been gathered into a band just above the elbow. A doublet with a low standing collar is worn open under the gown.

23 Anne Boleyn, 1533-6
Unknown artist

Note Although commonly believed, it is unlikely that Anne introduced the French hood into England after her stay in France. The earliest portrait of an English person wearing a French hood is that of Margaret Tudor, 1515-16

Head The French hood was a small semi-circular hood set on a stiff foundation and worn on the back of the head. The front border is edged with a row of pearls (referred to as a nether billiment) and curves forward on each side to end over the ears, thus exposing the centre parting of the hair. The back of the crown, edged with another row of pearls (the upper billiment), is raised in a curve. A curtain of black velvet, far narrower than that worn with the English hood, falls behind. A goffered gold gauze border rests on the smooth curve of the hair.

Body The embroidered border of the chemise is visible above the square, low-cut line of the bodice, which is decorated with pearl buttons alternating with pearls mounted in gold. The tight section of the upper sleeve is joined to the bodice on the shoulder line. The deep brown cuffs are made of fur.

Accessories Around her neck is a rope of pearls which has a pendant composed of the initial B and three pearl drops. The rest of the pearls and a thin link chain disappear into the bodice.

24 An unknown lady, c.1536
H. Holbein

Note It is possible that this cap would be worn under either a hat with a projecting brim, or a fur cap.

Head The lady wears a linen under-cap with a broad band of material bound round the crown and fastened at the nape of the neck. Extending over her ears and gripping her cheek is a side-piece which is probably strengthened by a metal hoop; to it is attached a metal clip the function of which is not clear.

Body The high-necked collar of the chemise is embroidered with an interlaced geometric pattern and a small frill is attached to it. The collar has been tied with two small bows. The fur collar and full sleeves of the gown underneath are just visible.

25 Henry VIII and his jester Will Somers, 1538-47
Unknown artist

Note Will is wearing livery of the Royal Household, which would have been issued from the Great Wardrobe. It is possible that he is wearing a 'base-coat' which was a plain jerkin with very deep skirts, mainly worn with livery or military wear. In contrast to Will's plain costume, Henry wears the elaborate style described in plate 19.

Head Will's hair has been shaved short and his is unshaven.

Body The hood of his coat rests on his right shoulder its fairly full sleeves taper to the wrist. The standing collar of an embroidered shirt has been drawn in around the neck. Over it the front-fastening coat has a pleated knee-length skirt that is guarded with velvet.

Accessories A simple girdle from which is suspended a pouch is worn round the waist. His black shoes have square-shaped uppers.

26 An unknown man, 1532-40.
H. Holbein

Note This man is probably a well-to-do tradesman who wishes to look imposing, an effect ensured by his trailing blue gown but his choice of footwear for the filthy streets is functional rather than decorative.

Head His hat is tied with a bow on top. It has a low crown and brim that projects at the front and is turned up at the back. He wears a moustache with a full, longish beard.

Body The high-standing collar of this tunic rises above the smaller one of his blue gown. Into the gown's collar are gathered the voluminous folds of the gown which trails on the ground behind. The broad shoulders of this gown have been cut to form a pendulous hanging section from which emerges the tunic sleeves gathered into a wristband and the drooping cuff of the shirt. Under the gown the knee-length tunic is buttoned down the centre.

Accessories A plain leather belt is fastened round the waist. The legs are covered with buttoned gaiters and the feet have been slipped into flat overshoes that resemble mules.

27 Sir John Godsalve, 1535-40
H. Holbein

Note A more opulent style of gown sleeve can be seen in the portrait of Henry VIII (19) and the Duke of Norfolk (28). The buttoned cap was not fashionable but it was popular with professional men and those living in the country.

Head Sir John's buttoned cap has a fairly deep crown with no front brim but side flaps which have been turned up and secured by a tie knotted on top of the head. His hair is worn to the nape of the neck and he does not wear a beard.

Body A gown with fur revers is worn unsecured over a doublet, the latter having a narrow turned-back collar and moderately sized tapering sleeves. A shirt is tied at the neck. The sleeves of the gown have a horizontal slit above the elbow from where the sleeve continues as a hanging sleeve.

28 Thomas Howard, 3rd Duke of Norfolk, 1539-40
H. Holbein

Note As he is wearing official dress, the Duke wears the appropriate headwear – a cap and coif. When he was imprisoned for treason in 1546 his Garter collar, containing 54 garters and knots of enamelled gold and a Great George set with diamonds, was confiscated and given to his opponent the Duke of Somerset: a similar fate befell the Earl of Surrey (47).

Head The Duke wears a flat black cap over a black coif.

Body The embroidered standing collar of the shirt is tied loosely at the neck. His doublet has a small standing collar that is edged with brown fur. Across the shoulders spreads the revers and massive fur collar of his gown to fall in a cape-like section at the back. The full upper section of the gown sleeve has been cut so that the fur lining is displayed and the cuts are caught with aglets. The sleeve continues as a tubular hanging sleeve from the elbow; the rest of the arm is covered with a satin sleeve that is buttoned at the wrist.

Accessories The collar of the Order of the Garter with the pendant George is draped across his chest. The Duke holds the gold baton of an Earl Marshall in his right hand and the white staff of Lord Treasurer in his left.

29 An English lady walking, c.1540
H. Holbein

Note A well-to-do middle-class lady bunches up her gown to avoid the dirt of the streets. Her clothes are plain but fashionably cut, the main point of emphasis being the head-dress.

Head The lady's hair is completely hidden by a linen cap on a frame understructure and a fine linen veil pinned at the sides and billowing out at the back.

Body A similar transparent linen partlet is pinned with a brooch. Her gown fits closely to the upper half of her body; its square neckline curves upwards slightly. The sleeves are also cut tightly and are worn with a turned-back velvet cuff. The skirt is pinned up to the waist girdle revealing a kirtle also pinned up at the front.

Accessories Woollen or linen hose are worn with square-toed shoes that have been cut low at the front and sides with a strap.

30 William Parr, Marquess of Northampton, 1540-3
H. Holbein

Note It has been suggested that there is a relation between this costume and that worn by the Gentleman Pensioners (they formed a bodyguard for the King and Parr was made the Captain in 1541/2), since they were required to wear a gold medallion round the neck and a hat badge, either one of which could be represented by the detail top left.

Head A bonnet with a slightly wavy brim hides the crown. It is bordered with ostrich feather tips and a single feather that droops over one side. The bonnet is decorated with a medallion, aglets and other small ornaments, the design of which is shown in a detail on the left hand side of the drawing. Parr's hair and beard is sparser than that of Baron Vaux (22).

Body The neck is framed by a frill attached to a partially open shirt collar. The wide upper section of the gown's sleeves have been cut into fur-lined sections joined with aglets. The lower sleeves are narrower and finished with a wrist frill. Holbein has noted that the upper section is purple velvet while the lower is of white satin. A front-fastening doublet of purple velvet is framed by the fur revers of the gown.

Accessories A medallion is suspended round the neck.

31 Simon George, c.1540
H. Holbein

Note The embroidery on the gown and ornaments on the bonnet point to the increased interest in surface decoration.

Head George wears a bonnet with a halo brim of the same type as worn by Parr (30). It is decorated with an enamelled spray of violas, an enamelled medallion of a saint, small gold ornaments – vases, crossed fishes and lozenge shapes arranged in rows – and an ostrich feather. His hair is shaped into the nape of the neck and a full beard and moustache is worn.

Body The standing collar of the shirt has been embroidered with cross-stitch and its ties have been left undone. The shirt is worn under a doublet that is embroidered with gold braid. A white collar, probably belonging to a jerkin, has been turned down over the gown, the full sleeve of which has been embroidered with a panel of interlaced cord decoration. The embroidered frill attached to the shirt sleeve falls loosely over the wrist.

33 Mrs Pemberton, c.1540
H. Holbein

Note Display of the embroidered undergarment is beginning to be an important focal point. Mrs Pemberton wears the restrained, yet elegant, dress of a country gentlewoman.

Head The headwear consists of three layers: first a frontlet, an ornamental band worn across the top of the forehead but revealing the parted hair; then an undercap that is clamped against the side of the face, and finally a small soft brimless bonnet.

Body The top tie of the standing collar of the chemise is left undone and the other two loosely tied. Her close-fitting kirtle bodice has a black velvet yoke against which is contrasted the white lining of the turned-back collar. The V-shaped opening of the collar is filled with a pair of aglets and a red flower. The sleeves closely fit the upper part of the arm and then expand into a wide bell-like shape, out of which emerges the embroidered cuff of the chemise. A linen kerchief has been placed over the shoulders.

32 Mary Zouch, 1540-1
H. Holbein

Note Mary's elegant and simple dress, relieved only by the ornate medallion, is typical of that worn at the court of Henry VIII in the late 1530s and early 1540s.

Head Mary wears a French hood on her smoothly parted hair.

Body The low curved line of the rigid kirtle bodice discloses an area unadorned except for a necklace. It would be fastened invisibly down one side and is edged with the border of the chemise. The fit of the upper part of the sleeves is extremely tight and contrasts with the full folds of the turned-back cuff.

Accessories A large oval medallion has been pinned to the centre of the bodice.

34 Catherine Howard (?), 1540-1
After H. Holbein

Note Catherine wears a sleeve that is an unusual shape for this date; the only dated parallel is that worn by the Duchess of Milan in Holbein's portrait of 1538 in the National Gallery, London. The pendant on the bodice depicts Lot's family being led away from Sodom. Holbein's original design for this piece of jewellery is in the British Museum in London.

Head On the head is worn a French hood of the later style. It consists of a white undercap that curves forward onto the cheek and is secured under the chin by a strap. The top curve is edged with a band of braid and a border of crimped gold gauze rests on the hair. A line of alternate spherical and rectangular cylindrical beads decorates the top of the hood. A rectangular curtain of black velvet hangs behind the shoulders.

Body Very full black velvet sleeves are pleated into the armhole of a close-fitting bodice of black satin with a black velvet yoke. The upstanding collar attached to the bodice is lined with white satin. The sleeves are open from shoulder to wrist and this area has been filled in with bands of gold embroidery caught with aglets and finished with a wrist frill of blackwork embroidery. A black satin overskirt is worn with a black-and-gold chequered underskirt.

Accessories A pearl-and-jewel necklace is worn around her throat and a large pendant is attached to the bodice. A jewelled girdle with a large pendant is just visible.

35 Henry VIII, c.1542
Unknown artist

Note Edward Hall writing in 1540 described this garment as a 'coate of purple velvet somewhat made lyke a frocke all over embrodred with flat gold of damaske with small lace mixed betwene of the same gold'. This loose garment suited the King in his last year as he became increasingly stout and immobile.

Head Henry's halo-brimmed bonnet is encrusted with jewels and is worn without the usual feather. He has grown his beard so that it has a gap in the middle.

Body The turned-down collar of the shirt disappears into the bulk of Henry's neck. Over it the fur-lined coat is embroidered with rows of narrow gold cords; it has been cut with sloping shoulders and sleeves that end above the elbow. They have been slit down the front so that their fur lining is disclosed. This area is banded by an interlaced pattern of braid and arranged across it are several horizontal jewelled clasps. The coat sleeves are continued as false hanging sleeves, while the doublet sleeves have been cut so that puffs of the shirt alternate with rubies set in gold.

Accessories A large gold collar of pearls and jewels is draped across the chest. In his left hand Henry holds a walking stick with an ornamental gold top and in his right, his gloves.

36 Lady of the Bodenham(?) family, c.1540-45
Unknown artist

Note This portrait gives a vivid impression of the contrast that was created when blackwork embroidery was set against a dark background of velvet and satin.

Head In this English version of the French hood the top of the crown is flattened across the head to turn wide of the temples and then turn in at an angle to end over the ears; it has upper and nether billiments. Her hair puffs out slightly from a tight centre parting.

Body The bodice collar is turned outwards to display its lining of blackwork embroidery and a narrow attached frill. The lady's tight-fitting

bodice with a velvet yoke ends in a deep V on a figured velvet forepart and smooth black satin overskirt. The bodice has a slightly less tight upper sleeve section, which is worn with a black velvet cuff and a very full satin undersleeve cut to display puffs of chemise embroidered with a stylized honeysuckle motif. Small bows decorate the cuffs and the wrist frills are embroidered with a smaller version of the design on the collar.

Accessories A simple chain is worn around the neck. A pendant pinned to the yoke depicts a seated lady with a lute and the words 'Praise the Lord for evermore'. A ribbon girdle entwined with a chain hangs down the front of the skirt.

ANNO DNI   1544.

LADI MARI   DOVGHTER TO
THE MOST   VERTVOVS PRINCE
KING HENRI   THE EIGHT

THE AGE OF   XXVIII YERES

48

37 Mary I, 1544
Master John

Note The bodice is beginning to assume the downward curve that ultimately becomes a pronounced V shape. Mary loved rich Spanish brocades and the stylized pomegranate pattern she is wearing here is typical of this type of material.

Head On her head she wears a French hood with a crimped edging and pearl-and-jewel billiments.

Body The low square neckline of the bodice, edged with pearls and the border of the chemise, fits closely to the body. The matching sleeves of orange and red brocade are worn with huge velvet cuffs and undersleeves of white damask that are cut into oval shapes outlined in black and caught with aglets; through these gaps is drawn the delicately embroidered chemise. The gentle curve of the waistline is defined by a narrow, jewelled chain girdle from which point the skirt expands into an inverted V-shaped opening which is masked by her clasped hands.

Accessories Two ropes of pearls are wound around her neck. To one is attached a triangular pendant and the other disappears into the bodice. A pendant set with square-cut green and red stones and pearl drops is attached to the bodice.

38 Elizabeth Cobham, 1544

Note This lady's dress is very old-fashioned for this date and it demonstrates the time lag between fashions that were worn at court and those worn by the country gentry.

Head She wears the later style of English hood, with the lappets hanging down. The hair is hidden by rolls of striped material and a curtain of material falls behind the shoulders.

Body The gown, fitting closely to the body, has a yoked bodice with a V-shaped opening that is filled with either the edge of the chemise or a partlet. The full sleeves of the gown emerge from the shoulder seam to finish in a turned-back pendulous fur cuff under which are the gathered undersleeves of the kirtle finished with wrist frills. Her skirt falls in voluminous folds to the ground.

Accessories A rope of beads with a tasselled end is attached to the girdle.

39 Lady Jane Dudley, c.1545
Master John (attr.)

Note This full-length portrait reveals that a new shape has evolved. The triangular shape of the bodice is balanced by the inverted triangular shape of the lower part of the body, the stiff smooth lines of which are dictated by the recently introduced Spanish farthingale worn underneath.

Head Lady Jane wears a French hood with elaborate upper and nether billiments of gold and pearl with a crimped border.

Body The low-cut and slightly curved neckline of the silver brocade bodice extends into a V shape below the waist. The narrow sleeves attached to the bodice are worn with wide pendulous cuffs of lynx fur and an undersleeve of crimson-and-gold brocade studded with pearls and gold braid. The bodice has been cut with a deep, lower curve from elbow to wrist and this seam is caught together at intervals with aglets. The embroidered chemise sleeve has been drawn through these gaps and is finished at the wrist with a frill. The silver brocade overskirt is lined with lynx fur and it is worn with a forepart that matches the undersleeves.

Accessories A necklace with pearl drops and a large pendant hangs round her neck and a narrower jewelled chain disappears into the bodice. From a jewelled girdle placed around the lower edge of the bodice hangs a chain of antique cameos with a red tassel at the end.

40 Edward VI, c.1546
Circle of William Scrots

Note The restrained and simple combination of brown gown, pink doublet and white shirt is in marked contrast to the elaborate and highly decorated version of these garments worn by Edward VI in plate 41.

Head A bonnet is set at an angle on the side of the head; a spangled ostrich feather is spread over it. Edward's hair has been cut short.

Body A frill attached to the shirt collar is gathered round the neck; matching frills are worn round the wrists. Over the shirt is worn a pale pink doublet that is lined with fur and fastens down the centre. The top garment is a high-collared gown of brown velvet with elbow-length sleeves and a white fur lining.

Accessories A single pearl suspended on a narrow gold chain hangs round his neck.

41 Edward VI, c.1546
Unknown artist

See colour plate between pp. 72 and 73.

42 Catherine Parr, c.1545
W. Scrots (attr.)

Note The decoration on this lady's elegant costume is typical of the taste in the mid-to-late 1540s for an interlaced pattern of gold braid or cord set against a darker background.

Head A bonnet with a halo brim decorated with a spangled feather and aglets is worn over a pearl-edged under-cap (similar to that worn by the unknown lady in plate no.24) and a pleated linen frontlet.

Body The kirtle bodice of red satin has a V-necked opening and a collar turned back so that it displays its white patterned lining and attached frill. Matching single sleeves are gathered into the shoulder seam and they are decorated down the centre and round the wrists with bands of metallic gold embroidery set on a darker red background and pairs of aglets. The chemise sleeve ends in a full pleated cuff. Similar embroidery extends down the front of the bodice, the cut of which is much fuller than earlier versions of the same garment (see plate 36).

Accessories Around her neck she wears a pearl-and-gold necklace set with jewels and a large pendant.

43 Princess Elizabeth, 1546
Circle of William Scrots

Note In this portrait of Elizabeth at the age of thirteen she is already displaying her love of sumptuous fabrics and jewels, especially pearls. The colour scheme of gold red and silver was a favourite one of hers as it complimented her red hair and pale skin.

Head She wears a French hood with pearl-and-jewel upper and nether billiments on smoothly parted hair.

Body The tight bodice of crimson cloth of gold damask has a low square neckline that is bordered with ornaments alternating with groups of pearls. The sleeves of the bodice have been cut very closely to the top of the arm and the turned back cuff slopes away to reveal the immense width of the undersleeves of silver-grey satin embroidered with a raised pattern in gold. These have been cut along the lower seam so that puffs of chemise caught by jewels can be displayed. There are chemise frills round the wrists. The bodice finishes in a V just below the waist-line and this is outlined with a jewelled girdle. A smooth flat overskirt of matching damask is parted over the forepart of silver-grey satin.

Accessories A pearl necklace and pendant are twisted round the throat and a large gold jewel comprising a black enamel cross set with diamonds and pearls is pinned to the bodice.

44 Unknown boy, 1545-50
Florentine School

Note This unknown Florentine wears an early form of trunk hose (see also plate 47). The combination of brilliant orange and black contrasts with the more sombre colours worn by the northern Italian nobleman in plate 8.

Head He wears a bonnet with a pleated crown and narrow brim which is decorated with jewels and a feather trim.

Body An embroidered shirt frill is gathered round his neck and the shirt has matching wrist frills. Over the shirt is worn a low-waisted doublet of orangey-red satin that is divided into panels by vertical lines of stitching. Each panel has been slashed at regular intervals. The black, fur-lined gown has revers and a turned-down collar; its sleeves have been cut down the centre to display the doublet underneath. The edges of the gown sleeves have been caught together with triangular jewels and decorated with bands of scrolling gold braid. Above the line of the belt the ties that unite the breeches to the doublet are clearly visible. The slashed panes of the breeches are gathered into a band just above the knee and the lining is pulled through the panes. The prominent cod-piece has also been slashed and puffs of its lining pulled through. He wears matching stockings.

Accessories He wears a narrow, leather belt and sword-belt. His shoes are flat with rounded and pinked toes.

Head His flat cap has a broader brim that has been pinned down on one side with an elaborate medallion; an ostrich feather has been placed on the other side. The hair is short and the man is clean-shaven.

Body The high-necked shirt has an attached frill which is embroidered with blackwork. The same pattern is continued as a border to the front opening of the shirt. Voluminous slashed sleeves of red satin secured with aglets emerge from the shoulders of the short gown to end in a scalloped edge above the flared frill of the shirt sleeves. Under the gown is worn a matching jerkin that has a low standing collar, slightly protruding belly and full, overlapping skirts the border of which is slashed. The upper hose have been slashed to display their darker coloured lining. Matching cod-piece and hose complete the outfit.

Accessories The narrow leather belt with dagger and tassel attached and the sword-belt draw attention to the slightly lower waistline. The shoes are closed to the ankle and have rounded toes which have been slashed diagonally and studded with tiny jewels.

46 Thomas Wentworth, 1st Baron, 1549
J. Bettes (attr.)

Note This treatment of the gown sleeves was also popular with women.

Head The bonnet has a low, pleated crown. Wentworth has a drooping moustache with a small, pointed beard.

Body The fur collar of the gown rises up behind the head and is continued as revers. The sleeves swell out on the shoulders to taper to a straight band around the wrists; they are guarded with velvet and cut from shoulder to wrist so that the fur lining, caught with aglets, is displayed. The narrow collar of the shirt with frill attached is worn open at the throat. Over it the doublet is buttoned down the front to a fairly low waistline.

Accessories As Wentworth was Lord Chamberlain he holds his staff of office in his left hand and his gloves in his right.

45 Unknown man, c.1548
Unknown artist

Note This costume is unusual in that it is entirely in one colour. The brilliant red forms a foil to the bold black embroidery on the white shirt. Shoulders have now attained their most exaggerated shape.

THOS. WENTWORTH
LORD CHAMBERLAIN TO
EDWARD. THE. VIth
ANNO DÑI
1547

PÆNSES. A
.BEEN.

ANNO·DNI·1546·ÆTATIS·SVÆ·29

56

47 The Earl of Surrey, c.1550
W. Scrots

Note Surrey was renowned for his extravagant taste in dress; he wears an Italian fashion (see plate 44) and adopts an Italianate pose (see plate 8). One of the charges at his trial in 1547 was that he wore foreign dress. He was found guilty of treason and executed. His spectacular Garter collar was worn by Edward VI at his Coronation. This is a commemorative portrait of Surrey, painted a few years after his death.

Head The halo brim of his bonnet is spattered with small aglets and is topped with an ostrich feather. The Earl wears a moustache and a full beard.

Body The fur collar of a full, sleeved cloak rests across the shoulders. Nestling closely around his neck is the gathered frill of his shirt. A doublet with a much lower waistline and a slightly swollen appearance has very short skirts and straight sleeves worn with wrist frills. Its surface is decorated with an intricate pattern of gold braid that encircles areas of velvet appliqué. The cod-piece matches breeches that are an early form of trunk hose for the breech, paned diagonally, is distended in an oval shape from the fork to be closed at mid-thigh with two bands of matching material.

Accessories He wears the collar of the Order of the Garter across his chest and the Garter of the Order is fastened below his left knee. He also wears a belt with dagger attached and a sword-belt. Gloves with a hanging cuff are held in his right hand. The shoes have slightly splayed-out and slashed uppers and a shaped heel is just discernible.

48 Elenora of Toledo, c.1550
A. Bronzino

Note Elenora's magnificent state dress illustrates the fusion between Spanish and Italian fashion. When her tomb was opened in 1857 it was found that she had been buried in this dress, the striking pattern of the velvet brocade still discernible after 300 years.

Head She wears a gold caul criss-crossed with pearls.

Body A gold braid partlet studded with pearls fills in both sides of the square neckline. The embroidered edge of a chemise projects above the line of the brown, black and white brocade velvet bodice. It is cut closely to the body and has a central pomegranate motif that is worked in gilt loops surrounded by ogival bands. On the shoulders are wings which have been slashed to show puffs of the chemise; the sleeves have been cut in braid-edged panes with the chemise pulled through and caught with jewels. The sleeves are finished with the ample turned-back cuffs of the chemise.

Accessories Around her throat is a pearl necklace with a large pendant and another rope of pearls is draped across the bodice. She holds a handkerchief in her right hand.

49 Mary I, 1550-5
H. Eworth

Note From about 1545 to 1550 the one-piece gown worn over the kirtle becomes less important, though it is retained as an overgarment. Female dress now consists of two distinct parts – a stiffened bodice and a skirt the rigid shape of which was dictated by the farthingale underneath.

Head Mary wears the English version of the French hood.

Body The face is framed by a gathered frill attached to the embroidered standing collar which is closed by a jewelled carcenet. It is difficult to tell whether this collar is attached to the chemise or the partlet, as both were worn to fill in the V-shaped opening of the high-necked bodice. The yoke of the black velvet bodice has an upstanding collar, lined with white satin and trimmed with cutwork and worn half-opened and slightly turned back. The black satin sleeves, fitting closely to the upper arm, are replaced at the elbow with pendant cuffs of black velvet. The red satin undersleeves are trimmed along the bottom seam with gold cutwork and pairs of aglets and gathered into a jewelled band around the wrist, where a cutwork frill flares out over the embroidered frill of the chemise sleeve. Rectangular embroidered bands with aglets top and bottom trim these sleeves. A matching black skirt, worn over a Spanish farthingale, is parted over a red satin forepart.

Accessories A large medallion has been pinned to the yoke of the bodice and a Book of Hours is suspended from the chain girdle.

50 Lady Jane Dudley (?), c.1555
Unknown artist

Note Contrasting the dark material of the gown with a soft fur lining was a fashion that appears in many portraits of the 1550s and 1560s. From c.1560 the fur collar tends to become a more dominant feature rising up round the back of the head to form a frame for the face.

Head Lady Jane wears a plain black French hood of the same style as that worn by Lady Dacre in plate 52.

Body The gathered frill attached to the standing collar of the chemise is pulled in round the neck. The white fur collar of the gown rests on the shoulders and the puff sleeves of the gown are slit to show their fur lining. The lining is also displayed down the centre of the gown and around the vertical slits.

51 Henry, Lord Maltravers, c.1555
After H. Eworth (?)

Note The Spanish cloak, formed out of three-quarters of a circle, produced many voluminous folds. Its popularity remained for the rest of the century and demonstrates the influence that Spain had on English fashion.

Head A black velvet bonnet with gold buttons and trimmed with an ostrich feather.

Body A small ruff rests on the pickadil edge of the jerkin, the standing collar of which is closed with four buttons. The jerkin is embroidered with braid and curves into a low waistline; lines of braid alternate with panels of star-shaped cuts. The skirt is parted above the cod-piece and is finished in pickadil. Over the shoulders is a black Spanish cloak with a long velvet hood studded with gold buttons. Its ermine lining is turned back to form revers and a deep collar. The trunk hose are fairly loose and full.

Accessories A narrow belt and sword-belt.

52 Mary Neville, Lady Dacre, 1554-5
H. Eworth

Note The sombre costume worn by the widowed Lady Dacre is enlivened by the striking embroidered pattern of pinks enclosed within a coiling black line on the chemise and gown. The fashionable practice of wearing a nosegay of fresh flowers infuriated Philip Stubbes who assumed they were worn so that their lovers could 'catch at them'. A portrait of Lady Dacre's late husband, originally painted by Holbein, and now lost, hangs on the wall. It is dated 1540 and he wears the fashionable dress of that date.

Head A black hood is tied under the chin with a thin strap.

Body One hook of the standing collar of the chemise is caught in an eye; the other hook and eye are left undone. The top edge of the collar is turned down. A loose black gown falls in ample folds and is fastened down the front with tied bows. Its collar has been turned back to reveal an embroidered lining and attached frill. The puffed-out upper section of the gown sleeve divides in two at the elbow into a straight sleeve, finished with the frill of the chemise and a tapering hanging sleeve.

Accessories A black bead necklace is just visible around her neck and a fur stole has been draped over her shoulders.

53 Jane Ingleton, 1557

Note This lady's dress is simple but the cut is fashionable.

Head A French hood, worn over a coif, has been wired so that it curves onto the cheeks and completely hides the hair.

Body The chemise frill has been turned down round the neck. It is worn with a loose gown with a flat collar. The gown falls in folds from the shoulders and is tied down the front with bows but it diverges from the bottom tie to show the skirt underneath. The puffed-out upper section of the sleeve is slashed and a tubular hanging sleeve is attached to it. Straight undersleeves have been decorated with bands of material and finished with wrist frills.

Accessories A prayer book is suspended from the girdle. Plain square-toed shoes are worn.

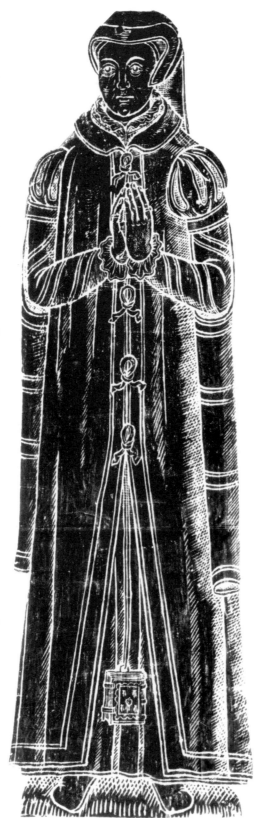

54 Sir John Gage and his wife, 1557

Note Lady Gage wears a costume almost identical to that worn by an unknown 61-year-old lady painted by Hans Eworth in 1558. It was typical of older married women living in the country far from the centre of fashion to wear a costume that was fashionable twenty-five to thirty years earlier.

Head Lady Gage wears a modified version of the early style of English hood. The curtain of material has been tucked in either side of the structure.

Body The collar of the close-fitting bodice is turned back to reveal a standing collar and the attached frill. The bodice, cut with a yoke, slopes into a gently curving waistline into which are gathered the heavy pleats of the matching skirt. The undersleeves emerge from the turned-back cuffs and are cut along the lower curved seam with the puffs of the chemise pulled through. Sir John wears a fashionable pleated ruff with his armour and a collar of the Order the Garter.

Accessories Lady Gage wears a thick chain necklace and chain girdle. There is a fur stole draped over her shoulders.

55 Unknown lady, 1557
H. Eworth

Note A thick chain twisted into a knot was an equally fashionable accessory for men. The frill is increasingly becoming a decorative feature.

Head A French hood with upper and nether billiments is worn with hair that puffs out on either side from a centre parting.

Body The embroidered edges of the chemise are tightly gathered round the neck. A loose gown falls from the shoulders and is fastened down the front with ties. Across the surface of the gown and sleeves are bands of fur that have been arranged in a regular pattern. Under the short puffed out sleeves of the gown are straight sleeves that are decorated with a gold-and-black strapwork embroidered pattern with each compartment enclosing an acorn motif.

56 Queen Mary and King Philip II of Spain, 1558
Unknown artist.

Note Features of Spanish dress that were imitated after Philip's visit to England were the vertical slashing on the jerkin and the use of dark colours set off by white linen at the throat and wrists.

Head Mary wears the English variation of the French hood and Philip wears a bonnet with a jewelled band around the crown and a small feather trim.

Body The frill attached to Mary's chemise has been turned down slightly. Under it the upstanding and lined collar of the bodice is worn open and turned back. Deep cuffs of squirrel fur are worn with undersleeves of gold brocade cut to show the chemise. The closely fitting bodice ends in a V shape just below the waistline. Her skirt has been parted to show a forepart that matches the undersleeves. The pleated frill attached to Philip's shirt rests on top of the standing collar of his jerkin which has a slashed puff on the shoulder and a hanging sleeve. The doublet sleeves are decorated with bands of small vertical slashes. Three very deep slashes and a scattering of small ornaments decorate the front of the jerkin. Its long skirts fall over the cod-piece and paned trunk hose.

Accessories Mary wears a jewelled carcenet and girdle. Philip wears the collar of the Order of the Golden Fleece and slashed shoes.

57 Lady Jane Dorner, c.1560
A. Mor

Note As one of Queen Mary's ladies-in-waiting Jane was presented to Philip and his entourage. She subsequently married the Duke of Feria and went to Spain with him. In this portrait she wears fashionable Spanish dress.

Head Her puffed-out curly hair has been intertwined with pearls, jewels and ribbons.

Body A close figure-of-eight ruff edged with bobbin lace rests on the standing collar of the bodice. The wings on the shoulders are embellished with jewel-studded bows and a narrow hanging sleeve is striped with lines of braid. Straight satin undersleeves are finished at the wrist with a double ruff and bracelet. Her bodice fits to the waistline where it ends in a tabbed border edged with braid and there are deep vertical slashes down the front. The surface and wings are covered with jewel-studded bows. The front of the matching skirt is fastened with bows.

Accessories She has a long drop earring in her right ear. A wreath of flowers has been wound around her left arm and a chain girdle with pomander is suspended from her waist.

lower billiment is studded with pearls and edged with gold braid; the upper billiment is composed of large oval and rectangular beads.

Body The embroidered frill of the chemise has been gathered round the neck and there is a matching frill around the wrists. The close-bodied gown fits to the waist and aglets have been scattered over the sleeves, collar and front fastening. The gown sleeves' swollen upper section tapers into a band just above the elbow. Flamboyantly embroidered undersleeves are arranged so that tight bands alternate with puffed-out sections slashed to show the underlying chemise.

Accessories A large pendant has been attached to the middle of the gown collar. There is a chain girdle round her waist and gloves with embroidered cuffs are held in her hands.

59 Mary, Queen of Scots, 1560-1
School of Clouet

Note This portrait, probably painted prior to Mary's departure to Scotland from France, shows her wearing the sophisticated and elegant style of the French court. Her pearls 'like that of black muscat grapes' were a prized possession. When she was forced to sell them in 1567, Queen Elizabeth secretly bought them for £3600 and is seen proudly wearing them in Segar's *Ermine* portrait painted in 1585, now in Hatfield House.

Head A caul of dull black mesh with silver loops and a row of pearls front and back.

Body The high collar of the bodice is turned back to show its white lining; the edges of the collar are trimmed with silver thread from which hang oval spangles of jet. The yoked bodice and sleeves of pinky-red satin are covered with perpendicular double rows of silver braid with groups of three tiny silver balls set closely in the intermediate spaces.

Accessories She wears white pearl earrings and her rope of famous black pearls knotted in front.

58 Unknown lady, 1560
H. Eworth

Note The complex cut of the undersleeves, the free-flowing style of the embroidery, the elongated aglets and the ornate embroidery on the gloves demonstrate the increasing pre-occupation with surface decoration.

Head The fashionable version of the French hood was the so-called Mary Stuart hood that favoured a pronounced heart shape. Here the

MARIE
REINE
D'ESCOS·
SE·

60 William Bullein, 1562

Note Bullein was a doctor and so wore the distinguishing coif and long gown of the professions.

Head A flat cap is worn over a coif which is bound with a scarf.

Body His shirt ties dangle in the opening of an ankle-length gown, the fur lining of which has been turned back to form revers and a collar. There is a buttoned flap on the fullish upper section of the gown sleeve; the rest of the gown sleeve tapers to the wrist.

Accessories A simple belt with a pouch attached is worn round the waist. Bullein holds a walking-stick and on his feet are flat mules.

Ye shalbe led before Princes
and rulers for my names sake.
Math. 10.

61 'Twenty-two godly and faythfull Christians', 1563

Note The many illustrations of the dress of ordinary working people in this book show that there was very little variation in their attire.

Head The women wear a variety of linen caps, while the men wear flat caps. One man has a hat with the brim turned up (a similar style is worn by the gardeners in plate 94).

Body The women wear linen kerchiefs draped like shawls across their shoulders and ankle-length kirtles with long sleeves. Some have tucked their skirts into their girdles for greater ease of movement, so revealing an underskirt. The men and the guards wear simple waisted jerkins with full skirts, narrow standing collars and straight sleeves. Their legwear is plain and simple.

Accessories Some of the women wear sturdy, thick-soled shoes. Close-fitting flat shoes are worn by men and women alike.

S^r.Nicholas Throcmorton

62 Sir Nicholas Throckmorton, c.1562
Unknown artist

Note Although trunk hose and breeches were usually made with pockets for handkerchiefs and other accessories, Sir Nicholas has chosen to wear a separate purse to accommodate his carefully arranged handkerchief.

Head He wears a bonnet with a curved brim and has a moustache and pointed beard.

Body An embroidered ruff is edged with bobbin lace. His doublet has a small standing collar and is buttoned down the centre to a low waistline, its deep skirt masking the hose. Matching sleeves emerge from wings on the shoulders and are decorated with alternate pinked bands that produce a striped effect. Three buttons and matching wrist ruffs finish the sleeves. A cloak is draped across the shoulders.

Accessories A pendant on a thin gold chain hangs around the neck. The elaborate purse containing the handkerchief is attached to the belt. A sword-belt is also worn.

63 Henry Stuart, Lord Darnley and Charles Stuart, Earl of Lennox, 1563
H. Eworth

Note At the age of six or seven a boy would be breeched: this meant that he would exchange the long skirts of his childhood for a scaled-down version of adult dress but this has not yet happened to Charles.

Head Both boys are bare-headed.

Body Charles wears a small ruff edged with black embroidery and a straight-sleeved long-skirted gown. Henry's ruff has been left undone and the ties have been knotted together. His high-necked doublet has a narrow double wing cut in pickadil and its straight sleeves are patterned with vertical bands of small slashes. The doublet is closely buttoned and slopes into a lowish waistline to which are attached narrow, divided skirts. Full trunk hose cut into panes is worn with matching stockings.

Accessories Charles holds a feathered bonnet in his left hand. Henry wears a watch suspended on a riband around his neck; round his waist is a belt and sword-belt and in his hands are a pair of gloves and handkerchief.

65 Theophila, wife of the 3rd Earl of Worcester, 1567
Unknown artist

Note Strong contrasts between black and white, small geometric-patterns and delicate bead necklaces were fashionable in the late 1560s.

Head Theophila's hair is dressed closely to the head and is hidden by a semi-transparent fine linen coif and forehead cloth.

Body The head is framed by the tightly gathered pleats of a small double ruff that is attached to a partlet embroidered with blackwork, beneath which can be discerned the top edge of the chemise. A close-bodied gown, patterned with line of small black squares enclosed within horizontal black lines, fits the upper half of the body to flare out in a bell-like shape that discloses the skirt underneath. The fur lining of the gown forms a bulky collar and it is also visible round the cut sections of the short sleeves. The white, tightly fitting undersleeves are patterned with rows of black oval shapes between dotted lines and finished with matching wrist ruffs.

Accessories A black tiny bead necklace is visible round her throat.

64 Elizabeth Roydon, Lady Golding, 1563
H. Eworth

Note Lady Golding wears a similar style of gown to that in plate 58. The collar in this example, however, is much higher as it rises up to frame the face. Chain bracelets were a popular accessory in the 1560s and 1570s and they closely resembled the modern version.

Head She wears a plain black hood.

Body Her ruff rises up round the face. The standing collar of the chemise has been left undone. A close-bodied black satin gown, guarded with brown fur, fits very tight to the waist, from which point it veers away. It has a high standing collar of brown fur and puffed-out sleeves that are closed above the elbow from where tubular hanging sleeves barred with fur fall. The undersleeves are decorated with a raised lattice pattern with a ruched section flecked with gold thread within each compartment. A wrist ruff is worn above a chain bracelet.

Accessories Thin chains are wound around her throat and thick, knotted chains are worn over the gown. She holds a pair of gloves in her hands.

20 Queen Jane Seymour, 1536
Hans Holbein

Note Holbein's portrait of the Queen is an invaluable record of the rich materials and ornate jewellery fashionable at the court of Henry VIII during the second half of his reign.

Head Jane wears the final variation of the English hood, a style in which the right half of the material was folded or twisted into the shape of a whelk-shell and then secured on top of the head; the remaining half of the material was allowed to fall behind the shoulder. The frontlet and tucked-up lappets are now shorter in length.

Body The close-fitting crimson velvet bodice, worn over a chemise, has a low square neckline that is trimmed with pearls and jewels. Matching sleeves cut tightly to the shoulder are joined by immense cuffs that are entirely covered with a fine network of gold cord. Wide silver brocade undersleeves emerge from these cuffs; their back seam is open but joined at intervals by jewels so that the chemise sleeve can be pulled through. A frill embroidered with blackwork and attached to the chemise sleeve falls over the wrists. The crimson velvet skirt is worn open in front to reveal a brocade forepart that matches the undersleeves.

Accessories A pearl-and-jewel necklace twisted around her neck has attached to it a gold pendant consisting of an oval emerald and a square ruby with pearl drop. She also wears a narrow, jewelled chain girdle and a large pendant attached to her bodice. This is composed of the black enamel letters IHS (Jesus) and is set in gold with three pearl drops.

41 Edward VI, c.1546

Note Edward's outfit is similar in most details to that of his father (35), though the waistline of the doublet is now lower and the shoulder line is sloping, rather than padded and horizontal.

Head Edward's flat bonnet has a band of jewels across the top of the brim; a white feather droops over the left ear.

Body The narrow, linen shirt collar has been turned down over the standing collar of a white-and-silver damask doublet that is buttoned down the front and bordered with a design of gold-embroidered squares. Below the belt the doublet skirts, now shorter in length, flare out over slashed hose that match the doublet sleeves. A red velvet gown guarded with gold braid and lined with ermine is worn over the doublet; its full upper sleeves have been gathered into the armholes to which are also attached tubular hanging sleeves trimmed with aglets.

Opposite

74 Unknown girl, 1569
Master of the Countess of Warwick, attr.

Note The late 1560s saw a preference for brighter, fresher colours set off by enamelled gold jewellery and gold braid trimming, strong naturalistic embroidered patterns and a distinctive arrangement of jewellery.

Head This girl obviously comes from a very wealthy family. Her velvet cap is decorated with feathers and jewelled roses and worn over a gold caul. A pink has been tucked in behind the left ear.

Body A double-layered ruff embroidered with gold embroidery is drawn in around the neck and there are matching wrist ruffs. Her partlet has a standing collar that is edged with gold braid and embroidered with the same pattern of red roses as the sleeves. The chemise can be seen underneath the partlet and V-shaped openings of the bodice, which has matching wings on the shoulders with puffs of the chemise pulled through. The tight-fitting red bodice fastens down the centre and its edges have been whipped over with gold thread. Panels of gold braid set on black have been used to decorate the front of the bodice. A skirt of matching material swells out from the waistline.

Accessories A narrow white sash serves as a girdle. Around her neck she wears a pearl-and-gold rope with a pendant of an enamelled gold figure. A pendant shaped like an oak leaf and studded with pearls hangs off-centre on the bodice with a thicker chain looped across it.

93 Sir Martin Frobisher, 1577
Cornelius Ketel

Note In this portrait of Frobisher the explorer, commissioned to commemorate his voyage to Newfoundland, he wears a practical but fashionable outfit.

Head The short hair, brushed up from the temples, is worn with full beard and moustache.

Body The single figure-of-eight ruff is worn above the standing collar of a buff-coloured sleeveless jerkin finished in pickadil on the wings and skirt. The jerkin is fastened with points and as the majority have been left undone, the closely buttoned doublet underneath is visible. This has fullish sleeves tapering to a closely fitting wrist section finished with a ruff. The points fastening the Venetians to the underside of the doublet are also visible. The voluminous, matching Venetians swell out from the waistline to be gathered in below the knee in a pickadil border.

Accessories His cream shoes have high irregularly trimmed uppers and slashed toes. He wears a ring suspended on a cord and around his waist are a belt and sword-belt. He holds a pistol.

Opposite

102 Sir Jerome Bowes, c.1584
Unknown artist

Note Sir Jerome was an impressive man, reputed to be 'three storeys high'. When this portrait was painted, he had just returned from a successful diplomatic mission to Russia.

Head The black tall-crowned hat is worn with a pearl hatband and white ostrich feather.

Body The lace falling band is worn with an underpropper so that it tilts. Draped across his shoulders is a green velvet, sleeved cloak that is heavily guarded with gold braid. His white satin doublet has a modified peascod belly; it buttons down the front and is decorated with horizontal lines of gold braid that enclose bands of vertical slashes. The panes of the pale green trunk hose are embroidered with gold. They are worn with white and gold brocade canions over which white stockings are fastened with gold-fringed garters.

Accessories Sir Jerome wears three thick gold chains around his neck. His green belt, sword-belt and hangers are embroidered with gold. He wears shoes of the same type as Sir Walter Raleigh (157).

Opposite

106 Lettice Knollys, Countess of Leicester, c.1585
George Gower, attr.

Note The Countess wears her most magnificent clothes and jewels in this portrait. The extraordinary range and density of applied decoration is typical of fashionable dress during the last two decades of the century. One of the motifs embroidered on her bodice and skirt is a ragged staff, the badge of her husband, the Earl of Leicester.

Head Her tightly curled hair has been arranged over pads so that it forms a distinct heart shape, the edge of which is trimmed with loops of pearl. On top of the head is a coronet of pearls ornamented with jewels and an ostrich feather.

Body Radiating out around the head to end in extended points are the deep pleats of a cutwork ruff. The matching bodice, sleeves and skirt of black velvet are encrusted with a snaking design of silver and gold embroidery, braid and sequins. Sequins have also been used on the bodice to outline its sharply curved border and elswhere to create borders. On the shoulders there are sloping tabbed wings from which emerge oversleeves lined with white satin. The right sleeve has been tucked into the lace cuff and left open to reveal the gold brocade trunk undersleeve but the left sleeve is allowed to hang free. The skirt, worn over a Spanish farthingale, slopes stiffly outward from the waist and is parted to reveal a forepart that matches the undersleeves.

Accessories Four ropes of pearls hang around her neck. A pearl girdle with a massive pendant attached has been looped up and pinned to the skirt. Another large pendant is attached to the left wing.

119 Sir Walter Raleigh, 1588
'H' attr.

Note Sir Walter's love of pearl decoration (see also plate 124) is well illustrated in this sumptuous costume of black and silver – the Queen's colours. His cloak would be secured by cords passing under the opposite arm and tied behind or around the arm.

Head His longish hair is worn with a curled-up moustache and pickdevant beard.

Body A triple-layered falling band of plain lawn is turned down over a doublet of white silk slashed in squares so that it has an uneven surface. Matching trunk sleeves are finished with a plain cuff. The doublet curves into a low, pointed waistline with large silver and pearl buttons down the centre. Its narrow skirt is covered with semi-transparent gauze. Black velvet paned trunk hose are embellished with alternate wavy and straight lines of pearls with larger pearls interspersed between. Draped over the left shoulder is a black velvet cloak with its sable fur lining turned back. The surface has been embroidered with sun rays worked in seed pearl, ending in a pearl trefoil.

Accessories He wears a pearl earring and a pearl bracelet. His belt and sword-belt are also embroidered with pearls.

137 Unknown lady, c.1595
W. Segar (attr.)

Note This lady's dazzling collection of enamelled gold jewels, black and white pearls and accessories enamelled with gold is displayed against a complementary colour scheme of black, white, gold and silver and this combination suggests she is wearing her finest court dress for the portrait.

Head Her hair has been brushed into a rounded shape with curls adding fullness to both sides of the face. The head-dress is an enamelled gold billiment studded with pearls and worn with a bongrace.

Body The deep circular pleats of an elaborate lace ruff radiate out around her head. Her white bodice and matching trunk sleeves have been embroidered with a coiling, interlaced design that encloses a variety of floral motifs and has been executed in blackwork, flecked with gold and silver. The sleeves and bodice are framed by a narrow sleeveless black gown that falls behind the bodice and skirt. This has minuscule tapered wings and hanging sleeves. The regular pleats of the bodice end in an extended point that is defined by an enamelled gold girdle and overlappng skirts, edged with gold braid. Her silvery satin skirt, decorated with dark-grey dotted ovals, swells out over the French farthingale worn underneath, with the pleats arranged so that a flounced effect is created.

Accessories Around her neck she wears a rope of black pearls, a rope of white pearls and a thin, black cord. Twenty enamelled gold jewels adorn the bodice; a further twelve have been fastened to the gown and they are also used to form a bracelet around the trunk sleeves. Two long, jewelled ropes of pearls, both black and white, hang down the front of the bodice. In her right hand is a fur stole ornamented with gold and jewels and in her left is a glove, from the cuff of which hang tassels made of gold beads.

66 Anne Browne, Lady Petre, 1567
S. van der Meulen (attr.)

Note Circular watches were worn as pendants at the neck or at the waist and could be attached to a girdle. They were, at this date, usually imported from southern Germany and were a rare and expensive accessory.

Head A plain black hood worn over a coif hides her hair.

Body The ruff is parted in the centre. The close-bodied gown has a high fur collar and a sharply curved upper sleeve section, while the rest of the straight sleeve has been cut to show its fur lining. She has matching wrist ruffs. The gown is close to the waist from where it is open revealing its fur lining. The outline of the whole costume is defined by a narrow border of black bobbin lace.

Accessories A watch is suspended on a riband around her neck. She holds a prayer book in her left hand and a pair of gloves with a pink attached is held in the other.

73

67 Mary Hill, Mrs Mackwilliam, 1567
Master of the Countess of Warwick (attr.)

Note The arrangement of the partlet or chemise with standing collar undone so that a jewelled chain is exposed was very popular throughout the 1560s. Enhancing the embroidered pattern on sleeves by wearing soft gauze oversleeves continued into the mid-1580s (see plate 108).

Head Mrs Mackwilliam wears a French hood with jewelled upper and nether billiments.

Body An embroidered two-layered ruff is tied under the chin and is worn with matching wrist ruffs. Her embroidered partlet is open revealing strings of gold beads. The wing of a sleeveless loose gown is cut with irregular slashes and the chemise pulled through. Straight undersleeves that match the partlet are worn with gauze oversleeves patterned with a small leaf motif. The black satin gown is guarded with velvet, and under it is a waistless underdress that is decorated with an interlaced strapwork pattern.

Accessories She wears a knotted pearl-and-bead necklace round her neck and holds a jewelled pomander in her hands.

68 Edward Windsor, 3rd Baron Windsor, c.1568
A. Mor (attr.)

Note Windsor has adopted the same pose as Sir Henry Lee (70) and he probably sat for Mor at the same time. In this portrait attention is increasingly drawn to the head as the curve of the gown collar and shirt rise higher behind it.

Head A bonnet with a low crown and miniscule brim is decorated with small, square and circular jewels and an ostrich feather.

Body The shirt collar, embroidered with bands of blackwork and its ties undone, is turned down over the buttoned standing collar of the doublet. The latter garment is pinked. The guarded cloak has a standing collar that rises up from the back portion with the rest of the collar forming a step and the front edge turned back as revers. Jewels have been scattered over the collar and across the shoulders.

Accessories A ring is suspended by a cord round her neck.

69 Thomas, 2nd Baron Wentworth, 1568
S. van der Meulen (attr.)

Note A jerkin worn over the doublet would follow the shape of the doublet. Slashes that extended nearly the whole length of the jerkin were a fashionable mode of decoration.

Head Baron Wentworth wears a black coif or skull-cap on the back of his head.

Body The strings of an open ruff have been left undone. A jerkin with a high standing buttoned collar has a curved, slightly swollen shape that is emphasized by very narrow vertical slashes and bands of pinking. It is worn over full, rounded trunk hose. A cloak with figured velvet revers is slung across his shoulders.

Accessories A narrow belt shaped to follow the curve of the waistline is fastened in front with a clasp. He also wears a sword-belt, and a black pendant is suspended on a riband.

70 Sir Henry Lee, 1568
A. Mor

Note Sir Henry was the Queen's Champion and in that capacity arranged many spectacular tournaments and other festivities to entertain her. The curious design on his sleeves and the rings attached to his clothes are probably related to this role.

Head He has a small, pointed beard with a neat moustache.

Body The single ruff has been left undone. The sleeveless jerkin has a standing collar and pinked yoke: the rest of the jerkin is cut into narrow panes from chest to waist. Shirt sleeves, embroidered with a design of interlaced knots and armillary spheres, emerge from pinked and slashed wings.

Accessories Thick chains are wound around his neck. One ring is suspended on a cord, another is tied round the elbow, while a third is tied round his wrist.

72 Countess of Warwick, c.1569
Master of the Countess of Warwick

Note The plain black gown, bodice and skirt is used as a background against which the Countess's prolific collection of jewels and intricately embroidered garments can better be appreciated.

Head The French hood has an upper billiment of enamelled gold and pearls.

Body Layers of an embroidered ruff encircle her face. The aglet-trimmed, V-shaped opening of the sleeveless gown has been filled in with a lawn partlet. Attached to the gown is a turned-back collar that is edged with aglets; the gown's prominent wing is cut and large puffs of the embroidered chemise pulled through. The undersleeves are patterned with bands of embroidery, encased in gauze and finished with a double wrist ruff. Tiny, star-shaped ornaments have been scattered over the matching bodice and skirt.

Accessories The jewellery consistes of a pearl-and-bead necklace over the partlet, a large pearl necklace draped across the shoulders and a delicate jewelled girdle. The Countess wears a spray of fresh flowers pinned to the gown.

71 Anthony Browne, Viscount Montague, 1569
H. Eworth

Note The doublet has begun to assume a curved shape, the beginning of a style that reaches an excessive degree of exaggeration in the 1580s and 1590s.

Head He wears a small bonnet with full crown and narrow brim, and a moustache with full beard.

Body The single embroidered ruff rests on the pickadil edge of the doublet's standing collar. Closely buttoned down the front, the doublet curves into a low waistline with skirts finished in pickadil and decorated with gold braid. The sleeves are straight and have matching wrist ruffs. The extremely wide fur revers of his gown are spread across his shoulders. The gown's short sleeves are decorated with aglets.

Accessories The collar of the Order of the Garter is draped across the chest. Montague also wears a belt and sword-belt and holds a pair of gloves.

73 Elizabeth I and The Three Goddesses, 1569
Monogrammist HE

Note Two goddesses wear the Renaissance version of classical dress of the type used in Franco-Flemish theatrical festivities. The third, naked goddess is seated on an embroidered chemise – the frill that is attached to its neck and wrist can be clearly seen.

Head Queen Elizabeth wears her Royal Crown, her two ladies-in-waiting wearing French hoods.

Body All the ladies wear small ruffs with high-necked partlets but the Queen also wears a ruby-and-gold carcenet. Her full state dress consists of a puff-sleeved, trained gown of black velvet, patterned all over with gold embroidery. Silver tissue undersleeves, encrusted with gold embroidery and pearls match the underskirt. The tight-fitting bodice has a long, pointed waistline that ends in a tabbed border. It is worn with a matching skirt that has been edged with gold embroidery and rubies set in gold mounts. The surface of this skirt has been cut to show its silver lining.

Accessories The Queen carries the Orb and Sceptre.

74 Unknown girl, 1569
Master of the Countess of Warwick (attr.)

See colour plate.

78

75 A workman, 1569

Note The workman wears a simplified, probably second-hand version of fashionable dress. The type of apron worn by tradesmen and craftsmen depended on the type of work in which they were involved. Carpenters and smiths wore leather-bibbed aprons, whereas butchers and cooks wore washable, coarse linen ones.

Head His hair is untidy and he has no headwear.

Body He wears a small ruff above the standing collar of a jerkin. Its double wings are in pickadil and the sleeves are straight. He has tucked his hands into the front-fastening jerkin, the deep skirts of which flare out over the full trunk hose.

Accessories The man wears a ragged apron and flat shoes with curved uppers.

76 A rich man and a beggar, 1569

Note The contrast between the dress of the rich and the very poor was, inevitably, very striking, but not all beggars were genuine. Some, called 'counterfeit cranks', pretended to be epileptics and would dissemble foaming at the mouth. Others wore fake blood-stained bandages to elicit sympathy from passers-by.

Head The rich man wears a tall-crowned hat with an ostrich feather trim. His beard and moustache have been carefully cut and shaped, whereas the beggar is bare-headed and his hair unkempt.

Body The rich man's sleeved cloak, casually thrown across his shoulders, has a standing collar and revers. It is worn with a buttoned doublet that has a tabbed border; the straight sleeves are finished with narrow wrist frills. The cod-piece is worn with paned trunk hose of the swollen, onion-shaped style. The beggar wears a short tunic that is ragged and torn. His legs and feet are bare except for a bandage.

Accessories The rich man has two chains round his neck and a narrow belt and sword-belt round his waist. The beggar holds a hat with a hole in it.

77 Four ladies. From left to right: 1. A London citizen's wife 2. A rich citizen's wife 3. The daughter of the first lady 4. A countrywoman; c.1570

Note Choice of dress was governed by one's status in society as well as by one's purse. This illustration comes from a history of the English, written and drawn by a Flemish refugee who has observed the distinctive dress worn by a group of London ladies.

Head The first lady wears a linen coif under a cap that has been wired into a curved shape. The second wears a cap that has projections on either side and is set on the back of the head. The third wears a coif and linen cap that has a fuller crown

and the fourth, a countrywoman has a chin-clout across her mouth and a high-crowned felt hat.

Body Ladies 1 and 4 wear their ruffs closed whereas ladies 2 and 3 have theirs undone. All the ladies, except for number 4, wear high-collared chemises and close-bodied gowns that have turned-down collars and straight sleeves. Their gowns are guarded with velvet and are worn over bodice and skirt. The richest lady (no.2) wears a brocade petticoat under her gown. The countrywoman has a kirtle with a front-fastening bodice, kerchief and long apron.

Accessories All the ladies either wear or carry a pair of gloves.

78 Unknown man, 1572
N. Hilliard

Note It is thought that the colours worn by this unknown man have a symbolic significance: the gold medallion on a green riband being a symbol of his love and joy, the black doublet and bonnet suggesting his grief and constancy, and the entire costume demonstrating his rôle as a suffering, but faithful, lover.

Head The crown of his black bonnet has been pleated into a narrow brim and is trimmed with jewels, a black ostrich feather and a single osprey feather.

Body The single figure-of-eight ruff, edged with bobbin lace, rests on top of the high-standing collar of the doublet. The shoulders of the latter slope away to a single wing that has been cut with diagonal slashes.

Accessories The man wears a gold medallion on a green riband edged with gold bobbin lace round his neck.

79 Sir Thomas Coningsby, 1572
G. Gower (attr.)

Note Experimentation with surface decoration in male and female dress in the 1570s took on an almost *trompe l'oeil* form.

Head Sir Thomas's bonnet, with a full, rounded crown and small brim, is decorated with wavy cord embroidery and small ornaments and a large black ostrich feather. His hair curls to the nape of the neck.

Body The closed ruff edged with bobbin lace matches the hand ruffs. The sleeveless jerkin worn over a doublet has a buttoned standing collar and narrow double wing; from these emerge straight doublet sleeves patterned with embroidery which is designed to look like slashing and pinking. The five vertical slashes down the front of the jerkin reveal the embroidery on the doublet, the skirts of which are fairly narrow. The panes of the trunk hose are covered with bands of embroidered dashes.

Accessories He wears a belt and sword-belt and holds a hawk lure in his right hand.

81 Elizabeth Littleton, Lady Willoughby, 1573
G. Gower (attr.)

Note Lady Willoughby's costume is highly complex and sophisticated. The proliferation of applied decoration is typical of the Elizabethan's pre-occupation with pattern and avoidance of plain surfaces.

Head She wears a tall-crowned hat with a jewelled hatband and spray of feathers over a caul.

Body Around the neck is a closed figure-of-eight ruff. The open gown forms one garment with the bodice, although it has a separate coat-like appearance. The gown has a stand-up collar edged with lace and faced with striped gauze. The full sleeves are composed of alternating panes of embroidered fabric and striped gauze caught with bows; the plain cuffs are worn with wrist ruffs. The square neckline of the bodice has been filled in with a partlet that matches the sleeves; a band of ruched gauze has been used to hide the join between it and the bodice. Sequins and braid decorate the bodice which ends in a rounded waistline.

Accessories A large pendant of Neptune is threaded though the ruched gauze, and ropes of pearls and jewels have been draped across the gown and bodice.

80 Lady Kytson, 1573
G. Gower

Head The combination of tall-crowned hat with gloves, worn, rather than carried, suggest that Lady Kytson is dressed for the outdoors. Colours and decoration are bold and striking.

Head Lady Kytson's tall-crowned hat has a jewelled hatband and large white ostrich feathers. It is worn over an undercap.

Body The deep, pleated ruff is worn over a transparent partlet. A vivid red gown with a striped braid fastening is wrapped around the body and to it is attached a wide, black fur collar that rises up from the shoulders to form a curve behind the head. The wings are trimmed with black-and-white braid and edged with black fur. The foliating embroidered pattern on the edge of the chemise is repeated on the narrow sleeves worn with gauze oversleeves, gold-and-black enamelled chain bracelet and matching wrist ruff.

Accessories She wears leather gloves, the cuffs of which are trimmed with red and beige bows

82 Two countrywomen, two fishwives and a water-carrier, 1574
J. Hoefnagel

Note All five figures would be a common sight in Elizabethan London though it is unlikely that the fishwives would wear their best clothes while working, as they appear to be, here. The water-carrier used his wooden container to transport water from the Thames and conduits into people's homes.

Head The two countrywomen wear wide-brimmed hats and chin-clouts; the fishwives have a coif under a shaped, linen cap.

Body The first countrywoman wears a small closed ruff, kerchief, straight-sleeved bodice, guarded skirt and underskirt covered by a long apron. The second lady wears the same but without a ruff. The fishwives wear small ruffs and close-bodied gowns with a puff on the upper half of the sleeve. The bare-headed water-carrier wears a simple, belted tunic.

Head The high-crowned bonnet is decorated with a bunch of feathers and a jewelled hatband.

Body James's closed ruff and wrist ruffs are worn with straight doublet sleeves stitched so that a ribbed effect is created. They emerge from a double wing in pickadil. The sleeveless jerkin, buttoned at the top, curves into a gently shaped waistline and has short, overlapping skirts. The surface of the jerkin has been decorated with horizontal slashes on the yoke and diagonal slashes on the rest. Green velvet Venetians, that are pear-shaped and gathered into the waist, narrow towards the knee where they are closed with a pickadil border.

Accessories He wears a belt and sword-belt and shoes with elongated and slashed uppers.

84 Queen Elizabeth I, c.1575
Unknown artist

Note The Queen's bodice has been cut like a man's doublet with a centre fastening, high collar and narrow overlapping skirt. The jewellery, unlike that in the Phoenix portrait (85), is not incorporated into the scheme of decoration, for the silk brocade does not need further enrichment.

Head A pearl billiment with a transparent veil attached is arranged on the top of tightly curled hair.

Body The neck is encircled by a deep figure-of-eight ruff. The matching sleeves, bodice and skirt are made of white silk, brocaded in a gold floral scroll design. The bodice is fastened down the front with buttons, flanked by frogging of gold and rose-coloured silk fluffed at the ends into tassels; it is fitted to a slightly pointed waistline with a narrow, tabbed border. The evenly arranged pleats of the full skirt spread out over the Spanish farthingale.

Accessories The jewelled girdle has an elaborate pendant on a black riband attached to it. Ropes of pearls are looped across the bodice and fastened to it off-centre. In her right hand Elizabeth holds a fan of natural-coloured ostrich feathers.

83 James VI, 1574
R. Lockey (attr.)

Note 'Venetians' were knee breeches that fastened below the knee and were available in several shapes – close-fitting, voluminous throughout (see plate 93), and pear-shaped, as in this example.

86

85 Queen Elizabeth I, c.1575
N. Hilliard (attr.)

Note The Queen loved to contrast lustrous white pearls against her favourite colours of black, silver and gold. The Phoenix jewel symbolizes the Queen's chastity and uniqueness; it was one of her favourite emblems and appears in different forms in her portraits.

Head An enamelled gold and pearl billiment is set on the back of her curly hair, and to it is attached a veil wired into a figure of eight.

Body The lace ruff that encircles her throat is worn over an embroidered partlet covered with gauze – the chemise edge just visible above the neckline of the bodice. The black velvet bodice, sleeves and skirt are decorated with a lattice framework of gold braid, studded with pearls, that encloses a gold, leaf motif. Converging lines of puffs emphasize the sloping V-shaped waistline. Swollen sleeves taper to a wrist covered by a lace ruff and a tiny chemise frill. The wings have been slashed and the puffs are caught with jewels. The pearl-and-jewelled borders of the skirt are parted to disclose the silver brocade underskirt.

Accessories Her jewellery consists of a pearl-and-jewel carcenet and a heavy, jewelled collar across her shoulders that has a central rose motif and a pendant of a Phoenix. She holds a white ostrich feather fan in her left hand.

86 Robert Dudley, Earl of Leicester, c.1575
Unknown artist

Note The Earl's intense love of finery earned him a respected position as arbiter of taste amongst the fashionable men at Elizabeth's court. Knights of the Order of the Garter had the option of wearing either the Great George with the elaborate collar of the Order (see plates 28; 71; 156) or, as in this example, the Lesser George on a jewelled chain.

Head The Earl's small bonnet has a jewelled band and an ostrich feather. His long pointed beard is worn with a moustache.

Body The high, standing collar of the doublet, edged with a pickadil border, supports a lace-

trimmed figure-of-eight ruff. The slashed and pinked surface of the salmon-pink doublet buttons down the front into a slight peascod belly. The matching sleeves emerge from double wings in pickadil embroidered with gold braid. The doublet skirt and cuffs are treated in the same way. The paned trunk hose is also embroidered with gold braid and the lining of a similar-coloured brocade is visible between the panes. The cod-piece has almost disappeared.

Accessories He wears a belt and sword-belt and the Lesser George on a jewelled chain.

87 The Queen out hunting, 1575

Note The status of members of the Royal Household can be discerned by their clothing. The middle-ranking servants wore livery with the Royal badge – an eight-inch gold Tudor rose – embroidered on their jerkins and doublets. Although the Queen has been hunting she has not discarded her farthingale.

Head All the men are bare-headed except for the groom on the right who wears a coif. The Queen wears a tall hat topped with a bunch of feathers, over a coif.

Body The grooms wear small ruffs over the standing collars of their sleeveless jerkins which are embroidered with the crowned Tudor rose and worn with full, paned trunk hose. The chief huntsman wears a ruff above the standing collar of his slashed doublet. It has a more pronounced wing and his trunk hose is more exaggerated in shape. The man on the left wears a plain, buttoned doublet and Venetians finished in pickadil. The Queen wears ruff and partlet with a bodice that is V-shaped. Her sleeves are open down the front and caught with three bows. Her skirt and forepart are worn over a Spanish farthingale.

88 The Keeper of Hounds, 1575

Note The Keeper of Hounds wears functional, not fashionable, dress and it is in marked contrast to that worn by his social superior – the Falconer (see plate 89).

Head He has a tall hat with a wide brim that has been turned down over the forehead.

Body The tunic-like coat is fastened down the front with simple ties. It has a short skirts, a turned-down collar and upper sleeves that have been cut into scallops and slashed. He appears to wear breeches that end above the knee.

Accessories His horn is slung behind him and his sword is attached to a belt.

89 The Falconer, 1575

Note Falconry was a sport enjoyed by gentlemen and so this man wears fashionable and expensive dress (see also plate 79).

Head The hat has a tallish, pinked crown, a hat band and a bunch of ostrich feathers.

Body The standing collar of the doublet is worn undone. There is a small ruff and matching wrist ruffs. The slightly padded doublet curves into the waistband. it has straight sleeves and two pickadil wings. One side of the very full paned trunk hose is hidden by a large tasselled pouch; the hose are joined by canions finished in pickadil and the stockings are secured by a sash.

Accessories A gauntlet glove with small tassel is worn on the left hand to protect it from the hawk's claws. The shoes have slashed uppers.

90 Three children, 1575-80
Unknown artist

Note Points were strips of ribbon, linen or silk, tipped with either aglets or ornamental metal tags and were used to unite hose to doublet. They could either be tied on the outside, as in this painting, or tied invisibly on the under-surface of the doublet. The children have forsaken their long skirts for a diminutive version of adult dress and have chosen, rather endearingly, to include their favourite pets in the portrait.

Head The two boys are bare-headed; the girl wears a network caul on the back of the head.

Body The boys' embroidered falling bands are worn over doublets that are buttoned down the front; their fullish, slashed and pinked sleeves emerge from a narrow wing to taper into a tight band and tabbed border. The points that unite their paned trunk hose to the doublet have been tied in a line above the doublet skirts. The girl has a closed, lace ruff and matching wrist ruffs. The surface of her bodice has been pinked and then decorated with intersecting bands of darker material, also pinked. The hanging sleeves of her costume fall from a double pickadil wing.

Accessories On each boy's doublet, a jewel attached to a ribbon has been threaded through two slashes. They wear narrow belts and one boy holds a bird. A narrow chain has been looped across the girl's bodice and she holds a guinea-pig.

91 Robert Dudley, Earl of Leicester, c.1575-80
Unknown artist

Note The limited range of colours – black, white and gold – create a dramatic background for the Earl's splendid Garter collar and its elaborate, enamelled Great George.

Head His bonnet, decorated with jewels set in gold mounts and a white ostrich feather, is set on the back of his head. His long, pointed moustache is worn with a square-cut beard.

Body The same jewels are repeated as a central seam down the sleeve of his black cloak (it could also be a short gown). It has fur revers and is guarded. The ruff rises up behind the ears. His high standing collar is attached to a doublet that is slightly curved in shape and decorated with bands of pinking alternating with lines of gold braid. His full, rounded trunk hose is worn with a cod-piece and the panes, outlined with white braid, frame the disclosed areas of gold satin lining.

Accessories The collar of the Order of the Garter has been placed across his chest. His belt and sword-belt are cream leather.

91

92 Sir Philip Sidney, c.1577
Unknown artist

Note A metal gorget could only be worn with civilian dress if the wearer had been on military service. Male dress is now distinctly curvilinear in shape.

Head Sir Philip is bare-headed and clean-shaven.

Body His ruff, composed of a vertical figure of eight in one layer, is worn on top of a gilt-engraved metal gorget and with matching wrist ruffs. The white leather doublet buttons down the front into a peascod belly with almost non-existent skirts. Decorating the doublet are alternate lines of vertical serrated slashes and horizontal lines of pinking. The exaggerated trunk hose has been heavily padded, os that it swells out from the waist to turn in onto the thigh. Black panes have been embroidered with a striking strapwork pattern executed in gold braid.

Accessories The black belt and sword-belt – the latter threaded through the panes of the hose – are outlined with gold braid.

93 Sir Martin Frobisher, 1577
Cornelius Ketel

See colour plate between pp. 72 and 73.

94 Gardeners, 1577

Note These two men wear the dress of the manual worker – a simple tunic-style garment called a 'cote'. Towards the end of the century breeches that covered the knee but were left open were worn with a collared sleeveless jerkin.

Head The hat has a tall, rounded crown and a turned-up brim.

Body The loose, sleeveless tunic is knee-length worn over a straight-sleeved undergarment.

Accessories A belt is worn round the waist. One man wears boots, the other flat shoes.

95 Gardeners, 1577

Note Gardening became a fashionable
occupation in the latter half of the sixteenth
century but not all gardeners dressed in the
same way. There was a clear distinction between
the dress worn by a gentleman gardener (the
man raking) and that worn by a manual worker
like the man on the right and the men in plate
94.

Head Both men's headwear is similar to that in
plate 94.

Body The man on the left wears a doublet with
slashed wing and slashing around the elbow.
The doublet has a small collar, buttons down the
front and deep, full skirts that are guarded. The
other man wears the same basic outfit but his
doublet has a round collar and simpler style of
wing and sleeve.

Accessories The man on the left carries pouch
and tools which are attached to a belt round his
waist. Both men have flat shoes with curved
uppers.

The picture here set down
within this letter T
A right doth shew the forme
of Tharlton vnto the: shap
When her in pleasant wise
the Counterfet expreste
of Clowne to eate of russet
and sturtups to i rest: bein

Whoe merry many mad
when he appeard in sight
The graue and wise as well as
at him did take delight: rush

The partie nowe is goue,
and closlie clad in claye,
Of all the Iesters in the land
he bare the praise awaie.

Now hath he plaid his pte
and sure he is of this.
If heim Christe did dicto liue
with him in lasting blis.

96 Tarlton the clown, before 1588

Note Tarlton was a famous Elizabethan
comedian. In this illustration he wears his stage
costume which is the easily recognizable dress of
a countryman. The coat would be made of russet
– a coarse homespun material. Startups (loose
leather shoes) were worn by country working
men until the end of the nineteenth century.
Contemporary literature records that Tarlton
also wore 'great clownish slop with the lugged
boot' (startups).

Head Tarlton wears an unevenly shaped cap
over his longish curly hair.

Body His coat has a simple V-shaped opening
and straight sleeves, only one of which is turned
back. His breeches are loose and baggy.

Accessories The belt round his waist has a
pouch attached. On his feet are shoes of rough
leather that reach above the ankle and fasten
with a strap called 'startups'. He plays tabor and
drum.

97 Jane Bradbuirye, 1578

Note A common feature of memorial brasses is the old-fashioned nature of the subject's dress. This lady's dress is also out of date as a fashionable lady in the late 1570s would be wearing an exaggerated style of ruff and fathingale (see plate 98).

Head Her plain French hood has a short curtain of material attached to it.

Body She wears a ruff above a partlet. The turned-down collar of a gown rises up behind her head. There are narrow wings on the shoulders of the gown, and its puffed sleeves taper to a small wrist ruff. The pleats above the waistline suggest the gown is a loose one. A patterned skirt is worn underneath.

Accessories A sash girdle is tied in a bow in centre of the gown.

98 Dame Phillippa Coningsby, 1578
English School

Note The silhouette is becoming fuller and
stiffer. The width across the upper part of the
body is accentuated by a tiny waist and the wing
no longer projects above the sleeve.

Head Dame Phillippa's hair has been brushed
smoothly into a rounded, smooth shape upon
which rests a pearl-decorated network caul.
Some leaves have been tucked in behind the left
ear.

Body She wears a deep, closed figure-of-eight
ruff with matching wrist ruffs. The very wide
neckline of the bodice has been filled in with a
partlet, beneath which the embroidered edge of
the chemise is visible. On the shoulders are
square-cut wings slashed with small puffs from
which emerge full sleeves decorated with bobbin
lace and hanging sleeves decorated with puffs.
The curved waistline of the bodice tapers into a
sharp V that rests on the skirt; down the centre
of the skirt is a line of puffing. Both bodice and
skirt are guarded.

Accessories A jewelled chain entwined with
ribbon is looped across the bodice. Chains have
been draped across the partlet and flower-shaped
jewels have been attached to the narrow girdle.

99 Mary, Queen of Scots, 1578
After a portrait by N. Hilliard

Note This later style of Mary Stuart hood does not have the same
accentuated heart-shape as the earlier version (see plate 58). Mary wore
similar headwear to this on the day of her execution, for an eyewitness
reported that she wore a 'vale of lawne . . . bowed out with wyer, and edged
round about with boane lace'.

Head The Mary Stuart hood is worn with a wired head rail that has been
edged with narrow lace.

Body Mary wears her ruff undone; its strings end in tiny pearl clusters.
The right-hand side of the collar has been turned down over the ruched
lawn partlet to which it is attached. The square, curved neckline of the
black bodice fits closely to the body and ends in a deep V shape over the
matching skirt which is worn with a restrained style of farthingale.

Accessories A delicate, jet carcenet forming the letter M is worn around
her throat. Ropes of dark glass links have been draped across the bodice
and pinned to its top edge. They are also worn as a girdle to which is
attached a cross with a rosary. An enamelled crucifix is worn on a black
band round the neck and in the right ear is a tiny black pearl drop.

97

100 Sir Nicholas Bacon, 1579
Unknown artist

Note Sir Nicholas was Lord Chancellor and Keeper of the Great Seal and in his hands he holds the insignia of these two offices, a staff and purse respectively. An almost identical purse has survived and is in a private collection. It measures about 14×15 inches and is embroidered in gold and silver thread on crimson velvet.

Body The figure-of-eight ruff is worn undone and its hanging strings end in tiny quatrefoils. His black patterned velvet gown has deep fur revers and short sleeves that disclose the satin sleeves of the doublet; the latter are finished in wrist ruffs. Under the ties of the gown can be seen the turned-down collar of the fur-trimmed brown doublet.

Accessories A dragon-shaped jewel is suspended on a blue riband around his neck. On the first finger of his right hand is a large gold signet ring bearing the Bacon arms.

101 Sir Edward Hoby, 1583
Unknown artist

Note As armour conformed to the fashions of civilian dress, the shape of the breastplate was dictated by that of the doublet. Hence the more exaggerated style that is worn by Baron Windsor in his portrait of 1588 (114).

Head Sir Edward's longish, wavy hair falls around a tiny earring. His moustache is rather sparse.

Body The elaborate geometric patterns of his lace falling band are clearly outlined against the black armour. Matching lace cuffs are worn. Pauldrons made of several plates curve over both shoulders; their leather lining has been carried beyond the edge of the plates and cut into a tabbed border. His arms are covered in armour with a separate section for the elbow. The breastplate has a peascod belly shape and its leather lining forms a narrow border over the short trunk hose.

Accessories He holds a basket-hilt sword in his left hand. His right hand rests on the helmet.

102 Sir Jerome Bowes, c.1584
Unknown artist

See colour plate between pp. 72 and 73.

103 Unknown man, c.1585
N. Hilliard

Note The hairstyle worn by this youth was popular with the fashionable gallants in the 1580s and 1590s. The informal style of dress suggests that he is wearing a nightgown over his shirt.

Head His curly hair has been brushed in waves off the forehead with one long lock of hair, called a lovelock, trailing over the left shoulder. He is clean-shaven.

Body The lace falling band attached to the shirt is tied at the neck with the lace continuing as a border to the V-opening. There are matching lace cuffs. Draped around his shoulders and pulled across his chest is a grey-blue garment lined with pink shag, which was a thick-piled cloth that could be dyed in a variety of colours and used for lining.

TANDEM SI

104 Sir Christopher Hatton, c.1585
possibly after C. Ketel

Note A full-length version of this portrait shows that Hatton wore red-and-gold canions, white-patterned stockings and black pantofles with this outfit.

Head Hatton's black velvet bonnet has gold jewel ornaments scattered around the crown, an ornate brooch and white ostrich feather. He has a moustache and full beard.

Body The white satin doublet and straight sleeves have braidings of red and gold with rows of pinking in between. A cloak of black velvet is draped across the shoulders and its surface is covered with pearls set in three leaves of gold. The doublet, buttoned down the front, curves into a low waistline – its skirt is now a mere roll. The trunk hose match the cloak.

Accessories A cameo of the Queen set in gold mount is attached to three thick, gold chains worn around the neck.

105 Elizabeth Sydenham, Lady Drake, c.1585
G. Gower (attr.)

Note Lady Drake wears her finest clothes and most splendid items of jewellery in this portrait. The curious arrangement of the sleeves was very fashionable in the second half of the 1580s (see also plate 106).

Head The wide front border of the Mary Stuart hood is trimmed with peaks of lace and pearls; there is a pearl drop in the centre and jewels are set across the crown. Elizabeth's hair is closely curled and puffed out.

Body Her closed, cartwheel ruff has been set at an angle. From the scalloped wing on the shoulder emerge the upper sleeves lined with brocade and scattered with aglets. The left sleeve has been allowed to hang free behind while the right one has been caught into the lace cuffs. The trunk sleeves underneath are covered with pearl-drop-encrusted gauze. Her tightly fitting bodice slopes into a deep V-shape and is decorated with narrow lines of braid and vertical

lines of aglets; these are also attached to its narrow border. The forepart matches the lining of the sleeve.

Accessories She wears a jewelled girdle, and a cameo set in gold mount is pinned to her skirt. Four ropes of pearls hang around her neck.

106 Lettice Knollys, Countess of Leicester, c.1585
G. Gower

See colour plate between pp. 72 and 73.

107 Mary Hill, Mrs Mackwilliam, c.1585-90
Circle of Gower

Note The ruff has now assumed its most
exaggerated and improbable shape. This and the
enormous width of the sleeves have caused the
lady to adopt a stiffly erect pose. There is a
marked contrast between the sophisticated
pattern of the brocade on the skirt and the
simple stylized shape of the appliquéd flowers on
the sleeves.

Head Her head-dress is like a French hood but
with a rolled front; it is edged with wired pearl
drops.

Body Around the neck is a huge, closed
cartwheel ruff. The trunk sleeves have been
decorated with lines of white puffs that alternate
with large white flowers with red-sequinned
centres. The cuffs are plain. The sharply curved
V of the bodice is followed by a jewelled girdle
and a strong vertical line has been created down

the centre of the bodice by a series of white puffs. Her skirt, worn over a Spanish farthingale, is parted to reveal a rich grey-and-ochre brocade forepart.

Accessories Three ropes of pearls hang down and her right hand is slipped through them. In her other hand she holds a black ostrich-feather fan.

108 Unknown girl, 1587
J. Bettes

Note This portrait demonstrates the discomfort that the fashionable lady must have endured when sleeves and ruff reached such an extreme shape. Similar examples of large-scale naturalistic patterns of embroidery can be found in many other portraits of the 1580s and 1590s: a sleeve-panel of blackwork with an almost identical pattern is in the Royal Scottish Museum in Edinburgh.

Head The girl's hair has been arranged over pads in order to create a broad curve that dips in the middle. Upper and nether billiments of pearls decorate the back of the head.

Body Her neck is encircled by a cutwork ruff that been tilted up at the back to allow the best view of its geometric pattern. On the shoulders, the wings are cut with puffs of the chemise pulled through. These wings and the tubular hanging sleeves have been embroidered with narrow braid and sequins. The huge trunk sleeves are encased in gauze and covered with large-scale blackwork embroidery. Her bodice fits closely and is finished in an extended V shape, its surface embellished with converging lines of braid and sequins. The matching overskirt is parted to reveal a plain underskirt.

Accessories She wears an intricate jet bead carcenet is around the throat. There is a black bead bracelet around the wrist of her right hand in which she holds a feather fan.

109 Unknown girl, 1587
J. Bettes

Detail of 108.

110 Sir Henry Unton, 1586
Unknown artist

Note Sir Henry wears his most fashionable
outfit to record his appointment as Ambassador
to the Low Countries in 1586. Cloaks were a
status symbol and were worn so that their
expensive decoration would be clearly visible
(see also plates 116 and 119).

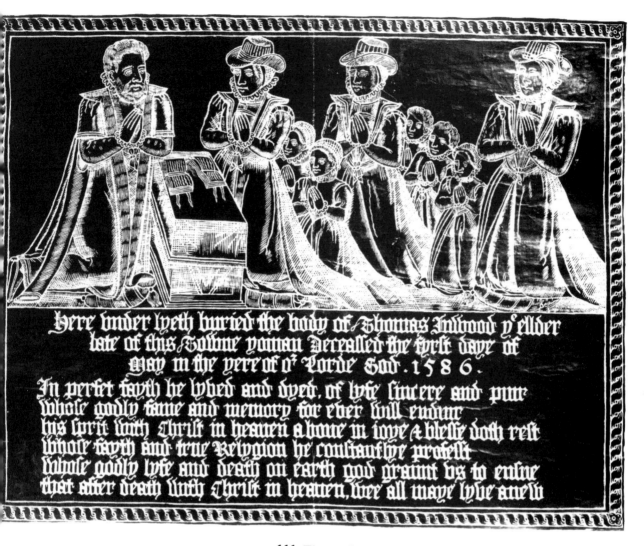

Here vnder lyeth buried the body of Thomas Inwood y ellder
late of this Towne yoman Deceassed the fyrst daye of
May in the yere of o Lorde God . 1 5 8 6 .
In perfet fayth he lyved and dyed, of lyfe sincere and pure
Whose godly fame and memory for ever will endure
his spryt with Christ in heaven aboue in ioye & blesse doth rest
Whose fayth and true Religion he conßantlye profeßt
Whose godly lyfe and death on earth god graunt vs to ensue
that after death with Christ in heaven, Wee all maye lyve anew

111 Thomas Inwood, his three wives and children, 1586

Head Sir Henry's hat has a high crown and is
trimmed with a pleated hat band, jewel and
ostrich feather topped with osprey. His hair is
longish and his beard has been cut in the
Marquisetto style.

Body A large cartwheel ruff encircles his neck.
Draped over one shoulder is a heavily guarded
Dutch cloak that has large ornamental buttons
set in the middle of tasselled bands of braid. The
white satin doublet has a simple curved wing and
matching, very full, sleeves. Plaited red-and-
white braid has been threaded through the front
of the doublet to emerge in a tagged bow on the
right shoulder. There are matching buttons
down the front of the doublet.

Note The conservative and old-fashioned dress worn by this family is
typical of that worn by fairly well-to-do people living in the country. The
'bowler' style hat was widely worn by country ladies and appears in many
other brass rubbings of this period.

Head The wives wear low-crowned hats with turned-up brims over
undercaps, and the girls wear cauls.

Body Both children and adults wear small close ruffs and matching wrist
ruffs, the wives with gathered partlets, the girls with the standing collar of
their bodices. Inwood has a long, fur-lined gown with short sleeves and
tubular hanging sleeves. The wives' gowns are caught in at the waist with a
narrow sash; the collars are turned down and the sleeves are plain.
Underneath they wear a bodice and trained skirt but without a farthingale.
The girls wear bodices with pointed waistlines and very full skirts whereas
the two boys have long-skirted gowns.

112 The Judgement of Solomon, c.1585-90

Note This embroidered cushion gives a composite picture of the exaggerated fashions that were worn at the court of Henry III of France (1580-9), many features of which were incorporated into English court dress.

Head The ladies wear heart-shaped head-dresses over their artificially padded hair. The men have curly hair that reaches to the nape of the neck, curled-up moustaches and the pickdevant style of beard.

Body Open fan-shaped ruffs and decorated trunk sleeves are worn by the ladies, whereas the men have the choice of either cartwheel ruffs or lace falling bands. Their padded sleeves are also pinked and slashed. The ladies' bodices are shaped so that they extend into a deep point that rests on their skirts, the shape of which is dictated by the French farthingale underneath. The first man (from the left) combines his very short, hooded Spanish cloak with extremely brief trunk hose, whereas the man next to him has a short collared cloak and brocade Venetians. A more elaborate outfit is worn by the man in the middle, for his peascod doublet and matching Venetians have central and transverse slashes with puffs of the lining pulled through.

Accessories Their footwear consists of pantofles, short leather boots and shoes with slashed and pointed uppers. One man wears a rope of pearls, whilst another has a large pendant on a riband.

113 Queen Elizabeth I, c.1588
Unknown artist

Note Pearls, whether tiny seed pearls or pear-shaped drops, are an integral part of the decoration of this costume and are included not only for aesthetic value but also as a symbol of the Queen's purity and chastity.

Head Elizabeth's hair has been raised over a wired support so that it widens out at the temples and dips slightly in the centre – a shape that is outlined with wired pearls. There is a jewel-and-feather ornament in the middle.

Body An elaborate and intricately patterned lace ruff encircles her neck. The ruff has been encrusted with pearls and is worn with matching cuffs. The lace edge of the chemise is visible over a partlet of gathered gauze. Massive satin trunk sleeves embroidered with a pearl-studded strapwork pattern that encloses honeysuckle, lilies and other flowers are framed by pearl-edged hanging sleeves. A matching stomacher ends in a deep V on a satin underskirt embroidered with flower roundels; over it is parted a black skirt whose tub-like shape is caused by a French farthingale.

Accessories She wears a pearl drop carcenet around her throat; ropes of pearls hang in front of the bodice and pendants have been pinned across its top edge. She holds a feather fan in the right hand.

Body The deep linen falling band has been embroidered with a coiling blackwork pattern of carnations, snails, roses and other motifs flecked with gold and edged with gold lace. Matching cuffs are worn over the armour. The surfaces of the gorget, pauldrons, central section of the breastplate, rerbrace, vambrace and helmet have been blackened and then etched with a flowing design of unicorns and arabesques. Gilt has then been applied to these areas. The breastplate is peascod shape and worn with fringed bases that have an appliqué pattern outlined with braid.

Accessories A heavy sword-belt embroidered with metallic thread, gems and pearls is draped across the chest. A plumed helmet and gauntlets lie on the table behind him.

115 Queen Elizabeth I, c.1588
G. Gower (attr.)

Note Curiously for a portrait celebrating a great national victory – the defeat of the Spanish Armada – the Queen wears a French head-dress and French court dress although the latter is without the customary V-necked bodice and wired collar.

Head The Queen's hair, probably false, is raised over a support and pearls are placed around the edges. At the back of her head is a small velvet cap with a jewelled ornament tipped with a pearl in front of a white feather.

Body The circular ruff is made from elaborate reticella lace. A vertical line of pearls and silk loops extends down the centre of the deep, pointed bodice. Pearl-studded hanging sleeves are attached to the massive padded wings of black velvet, their curved line followed by bars of pearls and loops of silk with emerald and ruby centres. The undersleeves of white satin are embroidered with red roses with pearl centres set in squares, and golden flowers set in hexagons. The pearl-and-loop-edged underskirt, worn over a French farthingale, is parted to reveal an underskirt that matches the sleeves.

Accessories A heavy gold collar and ropes of pearls have been arranged across the bodice. The jewelled girdle ends in a large bow.

114 Henry, 5th Baron Windsor, 1588
Unknown artist

Note Henry's magnificent set of armour is probably intended for tournament wear. The allegorical inset and pattern on the armour is likely to be the key to the device which would be painted on a pasteboard shield and presented to the Queen (see also plate 122). The Royal Armoury at Greenwich provided the finest armour. Suits made there for Sir Henry Lee and the Earl of Cumberland have survived, as has an album of designs.

Head Bare-headed, the Baron wears a moustache and marquisetto beard.

116 Unknown man, 1588
N. Hilliard

Note It is thought that this elegant young man dressed in the height of fashion and in the Queen's colours, black and white, is the Earl of Essex.

Head His hair is curly and fairly long and he wears a delicate moustache without a beard.

Body The closely gathered pleats of a cartwheel ruff radiate out around his neck. Nonchalantly thrown over his left shoulder is a short fur-lined cloak with fur revers. The doublet, that swerves into a peascod belly shape, is made from interlocking panels of serrated black-and-white material, and fastened down the front with ornamented buttons. The sleeves have been padded so that they have a swollen appearance and are finished with plain cuffs. Very brief trunk hose and white stockings complete the outfit.

Accessories A narrow belt is just visible above the hose. Hise white shoes have long pointed toes and pinked uppers.

117 Robert Sydney, 1st Earl of Leicester, c.1588
Unknown artist

Note Robert wears his scarf as an ensign of military rank. His mandilion, a loose hip-length jacket, is sideways in a manner that contemporaries referred to as 'Colley-Westonward', fashionable in this decade.

Head His curly, longish hair is worn with a small moustache and marquisetto beard.

Body His lace falling band is worn with matching cuffs. The upper half of his body is covered by a mandilion worn sideways so that the front and back panels cover the shoulders. One sleeve hangs in front of the body and the other hangs behind. Lines of braid and buttons have been used to trim the garment and it is tied by a lace on his right shoulder. Underneath is worn a doublet with full, pinked sleeves. The wide breeches have been decorated in same way as the mandilion.

Accessories Draped over his right shoulder is a scarf. In his right hand he holds a baton. The rest of his armour, a shield and helmet, have been depicted in the left- and right-hand corners.

INVENIAM VIAM
AVT FACIAM

118 Mary Huddye, 1589

Note This lady wears a very modified version of fashionable dress; neither her stomacher, farthingale, nor ruff have the exaggerated proportions that would be required in fashionable circles.

Head She wears a bongrace over a French hood.

Body Around her neck is a closed cartwheel ruff of modest size. Her bodice is worn with a striped stomacher front and sleeves that swell at the shoulder and then taper to plain cuffs. The material appears to be quilted. The skirt is worn over a small French farthingale.

Accessories Her shoes are thick-soled and closed at the ankles.

119 Sir Walter Raleigh, 1588
'H' (attr.)

See colour plate between pp. 72 and 73.

120 Giles Brydges, 3rd Lord Chandos, 1589
H. Custodis

Note Lord Chandos's hat with its high conical crown and brim turned up on one side is a Copotain, or sugar-loaf, hat made from block felt.

Head This high-crowned hat has a wide, twisted silk hatband to which is pinned a large jewel and osprey trim. He wears his hair short and has a curled-up moustache and pickdevant beard.

Body A falling band of cutwork falls over a doublet that is fastened down the centre with circular buttons. The doublet sleeve is decorated with diagonal bands of slashing and pinking and five ornamental buttons. A heavily guarded cloak is draped across the shoulders.

Body A multi-layered ruff, edged with lace is worn at an angle. The sloping scalloped wing on her left shoulder has a massive pendant depicting Diana and Aceton pinned to it. The entire surface of the trunk sleeves, bodice and underskirt have been embroidered with seed pearl in a design of butterflies and columns, and even the deep cuffs have been encrusted with embroidery and pearls. Her front-fastening bodice extends past the waist to end in a V on the black skirt parted to reveal the underskirt. A Spanish farthingale is worn underneath.

Accessories She wears a jewelled girdle around her waist. Ropes of pearls hang across the bodice, and another large pendant depicting Perseus and Andromeda is pinned to it. She holds a white ostrich feather fan in her right hand.

122 George Clifford, 3rd Earl of Cumberland, c.1590
N. Hilliard

Note Cumberland succeeded Sir Henry Lee (70) as Queen's Champion at the Tilt of 1590. Hilliard has depicted him in this rôle, for he is clad in his tournament costume and is in the act of challenging, with his gauntlet lying on the ground. The pasteboard shield containing his impress hangs on the tree.

Head His pale blue bonnet is surmounted by pale yellow ostrich feathers. The Queen's glove is attached to the turned-up brim which has been embroidered with the same pattern as the sleeves. The Earl has long, wavy hair, a moustache and pickdevant beard.

Body Over his blue armour studded with gold stars he wears a pale blue surcoat decorated with bands of gold and jewels. Its wide, short sleeves are turned back to disclose a white satin lining embroidered with celestial spheres and branches of olive. The surcoat has a square-cut neckline, peascod belly and knee-length skirts that are ornamented with vertical lines of jewels. His arms, legs and feet are entirely covered in armour.

Accessories A gold belt and sword-belt are draped across the surcoat. He holds a lance and his matching helmet and gauntlets are displayed around him.

121 Francis Clinton, Lady Chandos, 1589
H. Custodis

Note Lady Chandos's costume is an example of Elizabethan embroidery at its most grandiose. Its design is an unusual combination of geometric and naturalistic motifs. Her magnificent pendants, suspended by chains, have a cartouche-shaped frame in which is enacted a classical legend, the human figures and grotesques executed in enamels and jewels.

Head Upper and nether billiments have been placed at the back of the head and the hair has been arranged over two pads so that it assumes a smoothly curved shape with a dip in the centre.

123 Unknown girl, 1590
I. Oliver

Note Although the clothes worn by this four-year-old girl appear elaborate and restrictive to our eyes, she is nonetheless wearing a fairly comfortable version of adult dress with farthingale and stomacher omitted.

Head On her head is a Mary Stuart hood of orange-coloured network criss-crossed with black flowers.

Body Around her neck is a closed layered ruff of modest size. Patterned velvet sleeves with lace cuffs emerge from double wings on the shoulders. Guards of black velvet on the black satin bodice converge at the girl's natural waistline and the pleats of the matching skirt are tightly gathered into the waistband.

124 Sir Walter Raleigh, c.1590
Unknown artist

Note This splendid outfit would be worn at a tournament, as costume for such an event would be carefully planned, so that it created the maximum dramatic effect.

Head His hair is worn with a moustache and pointed beard.

Body A cutwork falling band is worn under a transparent pearl-studded covering. The pauldrons have a jewelled lining that has been cut into points. The breastplate curves into an exaggerated peascod belly and its lining is extended and decorated in the same way as the pauldrons. Pearls of different sizes decorate the very brief paned trunk hose.

Accessories The belt and sword-belt have been embroidered in the same way as the hose. The helmet has a massive plume of ostrich feathers which are completely smothered with pearls and then scattered with black stars. He holds a baton in his right hand.

125 Part of an embroidered valance, c.1590-5

Note This French embroidery illustrates the distinctive style of bodice worn at the French court. The collar of the bodice is continued as narrow revers that finish in a point on the skirt. The French cloak worn by the man is long and would be worn draped over one shoulder. This style of cloak was very fashionable in England.

Head The ladies have padded their hair out. The man has a soft, round-crowned hat.

Body The rebato worn by the ladies consists of folds of pleated lawn that fan out around the neck and are supported by a shaped plain collar fitted into the décolletage. The collar, outlined with lace, then descends to a point well below the waistline where it rests on the skirt. One lady's skirt has been tied down the front with bows, its full folds falling over a French farthingale, while the other lady's skirt is plain except for a hem embroidered with a scrolling pattern. Their trunk sleeves have either been slashed or worn open down the centre with the edges caught by a jewel. The calf-length guarded cloak worn by the man has a narrow collar and revers; under it is a slashed peascod belly doublet and close-fitting Venetians.

Accessories One lady holds a muff and the other a folding fan; she also has a mirror attached to her girdle.

126 Countess of Nottingham, 1590-5
M. Gheeraerts the Younger (attr.)

Note As a friend and confidante of the Queen, the Countess of Nottingham was an important lady at court. She is displaying her grandest court dress in this portrait. She wears the higher hemline of the 1590s and carries the latest fashion accessory introduced from France – a folding fan.

Head The Countess's closely curled hair is raised over a support and adorned with tiny horse-shoes of pearl and a head-dress of pearls wired into spherical shapes. The head rail, edged in the same way, is wired out behind the ruff, so that it curves into the shoulders and then falls to the ground.

Body Her fan-shaped, elaborately worked lace ruff ends in points and its join with the bodice is masked by a ruching of gauze scattered with pearl spheres. Trunk sleeves of black velvet are embroidered with silver spheres attached to stalks and leaves. The square-cut neckline of the bodice is extended into an exaggerated point and is decorated down the front with a puffing of gauze fixed with jewels. The skirt is similarly treated. Over the wheel farthingale is draped a black velvet skirt with borders embroidered in a

127 A courtier and a countryman, 1592

Note The text of the pamphlet from which this illustration comes criticizes courtiers for wearing expensive, imported fabrics and styles while the countryman is content with simple, homespun clothes and a corresponding set of moral values.

Head The courtier wears a tall-crowned hat with an ostrich feather trim. His beard has been cut in the pickdevant style and is worn with the customary moustache. The countryman's hat, probably made of straw, has a wide flat brim.

Body The exaggerated clothes worn by the courtier consist of an undone cartwheel ruff, peascod belly doublet unbuttoned to reveal folds of the shirt underneath, and baggy breeches buttoned just above the knee (they could be galligaskins). The countryman wears a loose coat with a tiny collar, baggy hose and loose leggings.

Accessories The countryman's accessories are functional – a pouch attached to his belt and sturdy startups. The courtier wears a belt, sword-belt and spurred boots that are turned down at the knee.

scrolling design of spheres and leaves. The heavily fringed underskirt is also visible.

Accessories Her jewellery consists of a carcenet around the throat, ropes of pearls that hang on either side of the bodice and a pearl girdle. Flower are tucked into the pleats of the ruff and a wreath of roses is twisted around her left arm. Her shoes have slashed, pointed toes and thicker soles than normally worn.

128 Queen Elizabeth I, c.1592
M. Gheeraerts the Younger

Note The rigid, heavily encrusted and totally artificial shape of late Elizabethan dress is exemplified by this portrait of the Queen, commissioned by her former Champion, Sir Henry Lee.

Head Pearls have been scattered over her closely curled, auburn wig. Perched on top is a crown-shaped head-dress of rubies and pearls surmounted with a pearl apex. Her wired head rail is trimmed with pearls.

Body The open, fan-shaped ruff rises up from the neckline of the bodice, the edges of which are trimmed with lace and jewels. Pearls and jewels have been used to frame the immense hanging sleeves that fall behind the trunk sleeves. The entire costume is made of white satin diagonally cross-barred with white silk puffings, the intersections of which have been studded with jewels. The long, pointed stomacher extends well into the flounce of the skirt, a matching piece of material that masks the hard line of French farthingale underneath. A very narrow brocade overskirt rests on top of the flounced skirt.

Accessories The Queen has an armillary sphere earring in her left ear and pink roses are pinned to the ruff. The jewelled girdle has a coral-coloured ribbon and a folding fan attached to it. A rope of pearls is knotted together in the centre of the bodice, while other ropes have been attached to each side. In her hand she holds gloves with tabbed cuffs. Her white satin shoes have almond-shaped toes.

129 Unknown lady, 1592
Unknown artist

Note The chemise could be worn as an alternative to the stomacher.

Head The lady's hair is arranged over pads so that it has a smooth shape. A bongrace projects over the forehead and there is a billiment on the back of the head.

Body Her close cartwheel ruff is composed of deep circular pleats trimmed with lace. The upper sleeve, edged with tiny aglets, has been split down the middle to display chemise sleeves of gauzy spotted material and plain cuffs. Her bodice has narrow revers of spotted material and the front is filled in with the gathered folds of the chemise.

Accessories Four ropes of tiny beads have been placed around the neck and flowers have been tucked into the pleats of the ruff.

130 Thomas Kennedy of Culzean, 1592
Unknown artist

Note This stylish 43-year-old man wears a style of Venetians that were an alternative to the pear-shaped ones worn by James I (83) and Frobisher's voluminous ones (93).

Head Kennedy wears his Copotain hat with its brim turned up on each side and with a richly embroidered hatband. His pointed moustache is worn with the pickdevant style of beard.

Body A plain falling band has been turned down over a sleeveless jerkin with hanging sleeves. The jerkin curves into a peascod belly, the line of which is followed by ornamental buttons. Underneath the jerkin is a doublet that buttons up to the neck and has trunk sleeves that have been decorated with regular lines of pinking and slashing. The buttoned slit in the left sleeve would be used as a pocket. The Venetians fit smoothly to above the knee where stockings are fastened over them.

Accessories A riband worn around the neck has a ring threaded through it. He wears a belt with a narrow looped chain and holds a glove with a fringed cuff in his left hand. Shoes without fastenings fit closely around his ankles.

Cortigiana Veneta

Cortigiana Veneta

131 Thomas Blunt, 1592
Unknown artist

Note A scarf tied around the arm in this manner indicates that it was given to the wearer by a female admirer. When it was worn by the military it would be draped across the body (see plate 117).

Head Thomas's hair is cut short and he wears a pickdevant beard with a rather sparse moustache.

Body A deep, cartwheel ruff encircles his neck. Although the doublet slopes to an extreme peascod belly, the cut of it and the sleeves is full. His extremely brief trunk hose has matching canions.

Accessories A tall, round-crowned hat rests on the table. Sword and sword-belt are plain in style.

132 Venetian courtesan, 1592

Note Venetian dress, usually made from a magnificent local brocade, was constructed on fairly simple, if grandiose, lines. The horned hairstyle was unique to Venice though it was copied elsewhere. Another curious feature of Venetian dress was the chopine – a leather shoe attached to a column of cork ranging in height from 4 to 18 inches. They were worn by the fashionable in England but were not of such an exaggerated height. The lady's profession is proclaimed by her undergarment, shaped like a man's breeches – at this time under-garments were worn only ladies of doubtful morals.

Head Her tight curly hair has been wired into two upright horns.

Body The open fan-shaped ruff is attached to the back of a bodice, the low, square neckline of which is worn over a lace-edged chemise. The rolled wing on the shoulder is surmounted with a standing semi-circular ruff. The brocade bodice curves in a peascod belly shape and the full stiff brocade skirt is gathered into a sharply sloping waistline. The view on the left shows that the lady wears knee-length slashed breeches and decorated stockings.

Accessories Her only jewellery is a pearl necklace. In her left hand she holds a handkerchief. Shoes with rounded slashed uppers are attached to chopines.

133 Henry Wriothesley, 3rd Earl of Southampton, 1594
N. Hilliard

Note A love-lock was a tress of hair grown long and brought forward from the nape of the neck to fall over the chest. It was the subject of much satirical comment.

Head The Earl's hair is brushed up from the forehead and the love-lock trails over the shoulder. He is clean-shaven.

Body The embroidered falling band, edged with lace, is worn open over a doublet of figured velvet flecked with sequins (or tiny pearls). His top button is left undone.

134 Sir Henry Slingsby, 1595
N. Hilliard

Note Slingsby's flamboyant headwear illustrates the enormous variety of styles that were available to men in the 1580s and 1590s. Conspicuous display of jewels on the hat was essential.

Head The tall round-crowned hat has a very wide, upturned brim of gathered satin to which an enamelled brooch has been pinned. His chin is unshaven and the hair is long and wavy.

Body A plain falling band, edged with lace, is worn open over the doublet. The doublet fastens down the centre and has a raised interlaced pattern that encloses small dashes.

135 A Spanish gentleman, 1601

Note Spanish court dress was not as ostentatious or extreme as that worn in Franch and England. Its main features were a high-crowned hat pleated into a very narrow brim, an ample draped cloak and fairly plain doublet and hose. This engraving has been copied from a costume book of an earlier period.

Head This gentleman wears a tall-crowned hat, a curled-up moustache and pickdevant beard.

Body Under a closed ruff the doublet is buttoned to a belted waist from where the full, guarded skirts fall over trunk hose. The doublet sleeves taper to the wrist which are covered with narrow ruffs. A full cloak is pulled across the body and thrown back over the left shoulder.

Accessories He holds a pair of gloves and wears shoes with pointed toes and slashed uppers.

138 James VI of Scotland, 1595
Unknown artist

136 Unknown lady, c.1595
W. Segar (attr.)

Note The costume worn by this lady has been adapted to accommodate her advanced state of pregnancy. Other portraits of women in a similar condition, but wearing far less comfortable clothes, have survived.

Head Her built-out hair is scattered with pearls. A wired heart-shaped head-dress trimmed with tiny gauze bows is set on the back of her head.

Body Her closed, semi-transparent ruff is patterned with small birds and finished in sequin-trimmed points. The bodice, skirt and white-satin sleeves have been embroidered with a scrolling pattern of leaves and stems executed entirely in pearls of different sizes. Plain cuffs are treated in the same way. Over the bodice and skirt is a narrow black gown with hanging sleeves.

Accessories Her pearl jewellery consists of earrings, necklace, bracelets and a thin black cord, twisted around her neck, which pulls up the ropes of pearls attached to each shoulder.

137 Unknown lady, c.1595
W. Segar (attr.)

See colour plate between pp. 72 and 73.

Note Although indifferent about clothes, James and his wife Anne spent an enormous amount of money on jewellery. The jewel worn in James' hat could have been designed by the Court jeweller George Heriot who accompanied James when he was made King of England in 1603. The spiky, jewelled spray above the crowned 'A' is very similar to Arnold Lulls's early-seventeenth-century designs for aigrettes. Lulls shared Heriot's workshop in London and his book of designs is now in the Victoria and Albert Museum.

Head James's tall-crowned hat has a brim that is turned up and caught by a massive jewelled 'A' surmounted by a spray of jewels set against an osprey feather trim. It is attached to a jewelled hatband.

Body A plain falling band rests on a satin doublet closely buttoned down the front and decorated in a herringbone pattern of thick braid, with the rectangles slashed. An ermine-lined cloak lies across his shoulders.

139 Unknown lady and two children, 1595
Unknown artist

Note While the children were toddlers, either
their hanging sleeve or a streamer attached to
the wing would be used by the parents as leading
strings. Children would wear caps called biggins
until they were about five or six and could also
wear a ribbed apron and a muckminder
(handkerchief) tucked into their girdle.

Head The mother wears a French hood with an
enamelled border and a bongrace. One child
wears two caps.

Body The mother's closed and layered ruff,
edged with lace, projects out over a sleeveless
gown that has serrated wings and scalloped
hanging sleeves. Her trunk sleeves have been
decorated in an intricate way – the lines of
closely looped braid frame irregular triangular-
shaped slashes out of which the contrasting
lining has been pulled. Her bodice ends in a very
deep point that is caught with a tag; its narrow
border has been cut into points and rests on a
skirt embroidered with inverted V shapes. Both
children have embroidered falling bands and
matching cuffs but the youngest has a bib that is
embroidered with little birds. Hanging sleeves
and loose full sleeves are attached to the striped
wings of their waisted and long-skirted gowns

Accessories The children have sashes draped
across their gowns and the child on the right has
a riband around the neck to which is attached a
rattle.

140 Unknown man, c.1595
I. Oliver

Note This unknown man wears the dress
appropriate for a fashionable melancholic
gallant. The colour combination of yellow and
black is significant as it symbolizes sadness at the
departure of a loved one. The lady that can be
glimpsed in the distance has the shorter skirt
length of the mid-1590s.

Head The unshaven man has a wide-brimmed
and square-crowned black hat on his long, curly
hair.

Body His embroidered falling band is worn
undone over a black doublet embroidered with
wavy lines of yellow braid. It has narrow wings
and straight sleeves finished with lace cuffs. The
doublet buttons down the front and has the
fashionable looser cut. Short skirts flare out over
brief black trunk hose joined by black canions.

Accessories He wears a silver-coloured belt
and long, close-fitting boots with lace-trimmed
boot-hose. On his left hand is a black glove. The
other glove lies beside him.

141 Detail from the life of Sir Henry Unton, c.1596
Unknown artist

Note This is the only picture of an Elizabethan masque in progress. It accords with documentary and other evidence that the chief features of female masque dress were long, blonde wigs or the natural hair worn loose, elaborate head-dresses and strikingly embroidered garments that could make an impact at a distance and in a candlelit room. Stomachers and farthingales were not worn. After the masquers had performed, they would engage the guests in a dance. The foreground circle of figures are masquers. Seated round the table are the guests at the banquet. The first figure in the procession is the presenter who hands a piece of paper to Lady Unton, the hostess, explaining the theme. Behind him come two torch-bearers, then

Mercury messenger of the gods, and Diana goddess of the moon and the chase. She wears a crescent moon in her head-dress and holds a bow and arrow. Torch-bearers alternate with six maidens in pairs carrying bows and garlands and it is these ladies who are described here.

Head Long blonde wigs are worn with a crown of flowers. Their faces are covered with red masks.

Body Grey-green bodices with square necklines are worn with white trailing skirts patterned with red flowers. They carry garlands of flowers and bows.

142 Unknown lady, 1590-1600
M. Gheeraerts the Younger (attr.)

Note The combination of loose hair, unusual head-dress (copied from Virgo Persica in Boissard's *Habitus Variarum Orbis Gentium*), draped mantle, absence of farthingale, striking embroidery sparkling with sequins and silver fringeing, and fanciful footwear, suggests that she is wearing masque dress. The mysterious setting and action depicted – crowning a deer under the shade of a tree – and the melancholic poem enclosed in a cartouche, are probably related to the device of a masque in which she appeared.

Head She wears her hair loose under a conical head-dress covered with ruched gauze and scattered with pansies. A streamer, edged with spangles, is attached to the top point of the head-dress.

Body A white, loose ankle-length gown is pulled across the body. Its V-shaped neckline has turned-back lace collar and the fairly full sleeve finish in lace cuffs. The surface of the gown has been embroidered in a circling design which encloses birds, fruit and flowers. The hem is edged with lace. Placed over the left shoulder and draped across the gown to fall in silver fringed folds is a silvery gauze overgown covered in spangles.

Accessories Her jewellery consists of a pearl earring with pearl drop, ropes of pearls wound around her right arm and a thin black cord around her neck from which are suspended two rings, one with coral-coloured stone and the other with a black stone. Her white-and-blue slippers are criss-crossed with pearls.

143 Elizabeth Vernon, Countess of Southampton, 1595-1600
Unknown artist

Note Embroidered jackets, also called waistcoats, could be bought ready-made in milliner's shops by the end of the century. They would be worn in the privacy of the home as shown in this unique portrait of a Countess caught in a moment of intimacy in her dressing-room.

Head The Countess combs her loose hair with an ivory comb.

Body The back seam of her jacket sleeve is undone and has been tied together with a series of pink bows. It has a turned-back lace collar and matching cuffs. The jacket has been embroidered in vivid colours with a pattern of flowers and insects and the bow ties down the front have been left undone. The hem has been cut into points and these edges embellished with hanging spangles. Her pink underbodice ends in a deep V and is laced up the front. To it is attached a gauze apron. The white satin underskirt has been embroidered with sprigs of blue flowers and its hem bordered with lines of spangles.

Accessories She wears a small pendant on a thin gold chain and a knotted rope of pearls around her neck. The pantofles on her stocking-clad feet are studded with pearls. Displayed on the curtain is a circular ruff with gauze ruching and beneath it a decoration for a stomacher that consists of a circling pattern of enamelled white flowers interspersed with black and red jewels set in gold. Her ermine-lined red mantle rests on a cushion and the rest of her jewels and pin cushion are displayed beside the jewel case.

144 Detail from the life of Sir Henry Unton, c.1596
Unknown artist

Note An Elizabethan baby's wardrobe consisted of a tailclout (nappy), a shirt, linen swaddling bound spirally over the shirt and a mantle. Swaddling would be discarded after the first year.

Head The ladies wear their hair brushed up from the forehead over a support. The nurse wears a Mary Stuart hood and the baby two caps.

Body All the ladies have ruffs with deep circular pleats. Stomachers are worn with the bodices and the skirts have been placed over wheel farthingales. Lady Unton has an embroidered gauze apron while the nurse has a plain linen one. The baby is encased in a mantle.

145 Robert Devereaux, 2nd Earl of Essex, c.1596
After M. Gheeraerts the Younger

Note The Earl's costume is typical of the preference in the 1590s for very pale colours – pinks, oyster and silver with a rich surface texture. Ruff and falling band were occasionally worn together from the 1580s onwards.

Head Hair is brushed off the forehead and the beard has been cut into a square shape.

Body A deep figure-of-eight ruff is worn over a transparent falling band. The spotted silver satin doublet has sloping wings outlined with silver braid and is cut in a looser style.

Accessories The Lesser George of the Order of the Garter is worn on a green satin riband.

146 William Burghley, 1st Baron Cecil, c.1596-7
Unknown artist

Note Cecil's sombre costume befits his position as an elder statesman and it clearly records his important position at court – Lord Treasurer and a Knight of the Order of the Garter.

Head He wears a tall-crowned hat with a cameo of the Queen pinned to it over a coif. A forked beard is worn with a moustache.

Body A single figure-of-eight ruff encircles his neck. His floor-length black gown has brown fur revers and is guarded on the wings and on the cuffed hanging sleeves and hem. The black doublet has plain sleeves and small wrist ruffs. Matching trunk hose, canions and stockings complete the rather austere outfit.

Accessories The Lesser George is worn on a gold chain and the Garter of the Order is tied around his left knee. In his left hand he holds the white staff of office of the Lord Treasurer.

147 Unknown man, 1597
N. Hilliard

Note This man is probably wearing a French cloak, a garment that was long, full and difficult to keep on and became a fashionable alternative in the 1590s to the short, rigid style of cloak.

Head He wears his hair long and curling over the shoulders.

Body A falling band with insertions of lace and a lace edging is worn undone over the doublet. The latter, its top buttons casually unfastened, has a projecting wing and sleeves decorated with bands of small vertical slashes. The shag-lined cloak has been pulled across the body and then thrown over the right shoulder.

148 The Browne brothers and their page, 1598
I. Oliver

Note Difference in social rank is indicated by dress. The brothers wear the latest fashion, whereas their page does not.

Head The brothers wear hats with flat crowns and narrow brims on their longish, wavy hair. Two have moustaches with a wispy beard under the lower lip.

Body The strings of the brother's lace falling bands have been tied together in front. Their black satin doublets have ruched folds and the looser cut follows the natural lines of the body and does not impose an unnatural shape upon it. The looser-fitting sleeves have curved wings and lace cuffs. The page wears a closed layered ruff and a cloak that is arranged in the same way as the unknown man (147). The short, gathered trunk hose worn by the brothers have matching canions and stockings that are tied above the knee. The page's doublet has been decorated with braid and pinking and is worn with hose of a different pattern and plain canions.

Accessories The brothers have embroidered belts and square-toed shoes that are fastened with a small bow.

149 A lady of the Talbot family, 1598
Unknown artist

Note The embroidery on the stomacher and glove which includes precious stones is typical of the most opulent type that would have been worked by a professional embroider. Examples of this type of embroidery have not survived owing to the practice of re-using the gems at a later date.

Head Her hair has been brushed up and over a wired support into a smooth, oval shape; loose tendrils of hair have escaped at the temples and jewelled ornaments have been scattered over one side of the hair.

Body The embroidered edges of a chemise are visible under the radiating pleats of a deep ruff. The square neckline that is disclosed by the open ruff is edged with interlaced network. Very rich embroidery worked in pearls and gems covers the stomacher. The Talbot-dog, a part of the coiling, naturalistic pattern, also appears as a heraldic device top left of the panel. Jewelled trefoils band the wings and the trunk sleeves, and the latter are finished in a plain cuff and bracelet.

Accessories An oval pendant is fastened to the ruff and a large pendant of a bird is attached to the left sleeve. Another pendant on a double chain is worn around the neck and chains hang on either side of the stomacher. A glove with an elaborately worked cuff is held in the left hand.

150 Lady Elizabeth Southwell, c.1599
M. Gheeraerts the Younger (attr.)

Note Elizabeth was the grand-daughter of the Countess of Nottingham (126) and was sent to court to be a Maid of Honour at the end of 1599. In this portrait she wears her court dress, certain features of which – the spiky head-dress, serrated hanging sleeves, open fan-shaped ruff and a colour scheme of white and silver – appear in other portraits of the Queen's Maids of Honour in the last decade of the reign.

Head Her head-dress consists of silver, fern-like leaves scattered with diamonds and other jewels and surmounted by a feather and is worn atop swept-up hair.

Body Her open fan-shaped ruff is composed of many layers each of which is trimmed with points of lace. The join between the ruff and the bodice has been masked by ruched gauze. Trunk sleeves of white satin have been decorated with clusters of pearls on wire stems set in oval compartments. They are framed by hanging sleeves that fall behind the skirt; their outer and possibly inner edges have been serrated and stiffened with wire, to carry projecting ornaments of pearls in groups of three. The stomacher matches the sleeves and is attached to a bodice

with a square-cut neckline. Her plain white satin skirt has been arranged so that the pleats radiate out from the waistline, to be folded under and around the rim of the wheel farthingale so that a flounced effect is created. A narrow line of braid edges the central opening of the skirt.

Accessories A long rope of pearls is knotted in the middle. The narrow jewelled girdle has a folding fan attached to it. Her pointed, white leather shoes have pinked uppers.

151 Edward Tollemache, 1600
Unknown artist

Note This doublet's extraordinary shape would have been achieved by excessive padding at the point of the waist, so that a bulge could be created that would overhang the belt and then curve almost to hip level.

Head His hair is longish and wavy and he wears his moustache with the fashionable tuft of hair under the lip.

Body Garlands and sprigs are embroidered on the falling band which has been turned over a doublet – possibly of leather – that has an incised pattern of flowers and braid-edged lines of pinking. Very full sleeves taper to narrow plain cuffs. The exaggerated peascod belly of the doublet droops over the belt and sword-belt and its narrow skirt is visible on one side only. The trunk hose are short and paned. Over his left shoulder is draped a cloak.

153 Elizabeth, wife of the 4th Earl of Worcester, c.1600
Unknown artist

Note Soft, shimmering fabrics embellished with sparkling embroidery, sequins or pearls were worn by the fashionable members of the Queen's court during the last decade of her reign.

Head Her hair is piled high over a wired support and there are tight curls on the forehead and at the temples. A bongrace is worn with a French hood.

Body Around the neck she wears a multi-layered, circular, lace ruff. The square-cut neckline of the bodice is edged with six jewels and jewels are also arranged in a vertical line down the front of the deep V-shaped bodice. Both sleeves and bodice are covered with loops of braid embroidery studded with pearls and the whole surface is covered with ruched and patterned gauze. The flounced farthingale skirt is of patterned satin.

Accessories There is a pearl necklace around the throat and a pair of plain gloves held in the left hand.

152 Francis Russell, 4th Earl of Bedford, c.1600
R. Peake the Elder (attr.)

Note The Earl's costume is of transitional style as it lies between the rigidity of the late 1580s and the softer, more natural line worn by the Browne brothers (148).

Head He is bare-headed.

Body The closed ruff has been arranged in a flatted figure-of-eight set. The doublet, hose and canions are made from satin with a small silk spot diapered over its surface. The doublet curves into a peascod belly; it has narrow overlapping skirts and matching trunk sleeves with undone buttoned slits and plain cuffs. He wears brief trunk hose with canions that finish above the knee.

Accessories Chains have been draped diagonally across his chest. A hawk is held in his gloved left hand. Almond-toed shoes decorated with pinking are fastened with a strap from the heel to the top of the tongue.

154 Queen Elizabeth I (?) c.1600
Unknown artist

Note Extraordinarily elaborate though this portrait is, it is not thought to be of the Queen. The convention of wearing an open ruff was reserved for unmarried ladies of the court. To wear a skirt material that contrasted with that of the bodice and sleeves was very fashionable from the mid-1590s onwards.

Head A coronet of pearls is on top of her wired, pearl head-dress. Pearl drops have been distributed over the built-up, closely curled and probably artificial hair.

Body The massive, multi-layered ruff composed of deep circular lace pleats is worn open, the join between it and the bodice masked by closely ruched gauze. A wired head-rail arches out on either side of white-and-gold damask trunk sleeves on which are embroidered pearl silk-worms. Jewels set in enamelled gold follow the line of the distended shoulders. Her very deep, silver satin stomacher is encrusted with vertical lines of silver braid and jewels that alternate with braid and sequins. The ochre brown satin skirt woven with a pattern of gold *fleurs-de-lis* is worn over a wheel farthingale and has a matching flounce.

Accessories A pearl-and-jewel carcenet is fastened around her throat. Pinned against a rope of pearls on her left shoulder is a huge circular jewel with radiating spikes. On the right sleeve ropes of pearls and red beads are attached by a red bow and she holds in her hand a pink feather fan. Many ropes or pearls are positioned on either side of the bodice.

155 Henry Wriothesley, 3rd Earl of Southampton, c.1600
Unknown artist

Note Southampton, the patron of Shakespeare, was well known for his sartorical style and is here dressed in the height of fashion with his elaborate armour arranged around him.

Head A sparse moustache is worn with a tuft of beard on the chin. A very long love-lock trails over his left shoulder.

Body His lace falling band is worn over a metal gorget with scalloped lining. Wings decorated with narrow lines of braid project over straight doublet sleeves. The doublet has a miniscule peascod belly and ends at the natural waistline; the skirts are deep and over-lapping. The late style of padded trunk hose is squarer in shape and its panes are encrusted with interlocking rows of braid. Stockings have been fastened over the loose-fitting matching canions with a tied sash.

Accessories Two bows have been attached to the belt which is worn with a matching sword-belt. His gloves have embroidered and fringed cuffs. His shoes are of the square-toed style worn by Raleigh (157). Matching breastplate and plumed helmet are beside him.

156 Charles Howard, 1st Earl of Nottingham, 1602
Unknown artist

Note The Earl wears the 'full dress' of the Order of the Garter – a costume that would be donned when the Knights made their annual procession on St George's Day to the Chapel at Windsor and on other ceremonial occasions. The Order was the most exclusive group of men in England, being limited to twenty-six men chosen by the Queen herself.

Head The Earl wears a black bonnet with jewelled hatband and ostrich-feather trim.

Body A closed narrow figure-of-eight ruff is worn over a plain linen falling band. On the right shoulder is the 'chaperon'. In medieval times it became a hood with a tail or liripipe attached but now was a symbolic circular roll, its tail placed diagonally across the body. The floor-length velvet mantle is worn over the shoulders and fastened with cords, the tasselled ends of which hang down in front. On the left shoulder of the mantle is embroidered the insignia of the Order and the white satin lining has been turned back. The crimson velvet gown underneath has short sleeves and is drawn in round the waist by a belt and sword-belt. The closely buttoned doublet is visible under the gown.

Accessories The broad gold collar of the Order with the Great George has been placed across the chest. He wears black shoes with slightly pointed toes and large spangled rosettes with white stockings.

157 Sir Walter Raleigh and son, 1602
Unknown artist

Note Raleigh wears the latest fashion – a black beaver hat at the required angle and both he and his son have the softer, less exaggerated style of dress.

Head The brim of Sir Walter's hat is caught up by a jewelled feather with a pearl drop. His curled up moustache is worn with the pickdevant beard.

Body He wears a small ruff with a collared, brown velvet jerkin that is covered with converging panels of silver and pearl. It has deep, over-lapping skirts and wings that project over straight, white silk doublet sleeves. The silver doublet is fastened with small buttons and is worn with paned trunk hose edged in silver, and pale buff canions fastened with white silk garters. His son has a plain falling band edged with lace, and a matching doublet and Venetians of turquoise-blue silk. His doublet sleeves are braided in silver and the surface of his doublet has been pinked. His stockings match the rest of his outfit.

Accessories Sir Walter's belt and sword-belt are of buff leather, embroidered with silver. Both wear square-toed shoes that have uppers ending in a small tongue over which the strap from the heel is tied in a bow.

Select Bibliography

Arnold, J., 'Lost from her Majesties Back', The Day Book of the Wardrobe of Robes. Costume Society Extra Series no. 7. *Elizabethan and Jacobean smocks and shirts,* Waffen- und Kostümkunde, 1973, Vol. XV pp. 109-24.

Byrne, M. St Clare, *The Elizabethan home discovered in two dialogues,* London, 1949. *Elizabethan life in town and country,* London, 1961. *The Lisle Letters,* 6 vols., University of Chicago Press, 1981.

Cunnington, C.W. and P. *Handbook of English Costume in the 16th Century,* Faber, 1962.

Digby, G.W., *Elizabethan embroidery,* Faber, 1963.

Gawdy, P., *The letters of Philip Gawdy 1579-1616,* I. Jeayes Roxburghe Club, (ed.) London, no. 148, 1906.

Harrison, W., *A description of England in 1578,* F.

Furnivall, (ed.) 1889.

Hentzner, P., *A journey into England by Paul Hentzner in the year 1598,* ed. H. Walpole, Aungervyle Society, Edinburgh, 1881.

Laver, J. (ed.), *Costume of the Western World,* Harrap, 1951.

Linthicum, M.C., *Costume in the drama of Shakespeare and his contemporaries,* Oxford, 1936.

Nevinson, J., *Connoisseur,* Vol. XCVII, 1936, pp. 25 and 140: 'English embroidered costume' Vol. CIII, 1939: Part I 'Unrecorded types of embroidery in the collection of Lord Middleton'; Part II 'English embroidered costume in the collection of Lord Middleton'. *Collectanea Londiniensia,* London and Middlesex Archaeological Society, 1978: 'The dress of the citizens of London 1540-1640'. Catalogue of English domestic embroidery of the 16th & 17th centuries, Victoria and Albert Museum.

Nichols, J. *The progresses and public processions of Queen Elizabeth I,* 3 vols, London, 1823.

Norris, A., *Costume and Fashion, vols 2 & 3. The Tudors,* J.M. Dent, 1938.

Platter, T., *Thomas Platter's travels in England in 1599,* Clare Williams (trans.), 1937.

Rye, W., *England as seen by foreigners in the days of Elizabeth I and James I,* 1865.

Strong, R., *Portraits of Queen Elizabeth I,* Oxford University Press, 1969. *The English Icon,* Routledge and Kegan Paul, 1969. *Elizabethan and Jacobean Portraits,* 2 vols. HMSO, 1969.

Stubbes, P., *Anatomy of Abuses in England in 1583,* F. Furnivall (ed.) for New Shakespeare Society, 1882.

Von Klarwill, V., *Queen Elizabeth and some foreigners,* 1928.

Winchester, B., *Tudor Family Portrait,* Cape, 1955.

Exhibition catalogues
Holbein and the Court of Henry VIII, The Queen's Gallery, 1978.
Hans Eworth, A Tudor Artist and his Circle, National Portrait Gallery, 1965.
The Elizabethan Image, Tate Gallery, 1969.

Glossary and Select Index

Note This lists costume and textile terms which may not be fully explained either in the text or the captions. The numbers in brackets refer to some of the plates where examples of the item listed can be seen. An asterisk denotes a colour plate.

Aigrette a jewelled hair ornament fashionable in the early seventeenth century.

Aglets ornamental metal tags that could either be attached to points or used in pairs with no visible tie and so could be used as a fastening or as a purely decorative trimming. (34) (41)* (58) (72)

Apron a linen or wool apron with or without a bib would be worn by the working classes and country housewives. Aprons without a bib and made of the finest material were worn by the fashionable lady at home towards the end of the century. (75) (77) (143) (144)

Band collar of linen worn about the neck of a shirt or smock. (6)

Bases lower skirt-like part of tunic worn over armour. (114)

Beaver the silky fur of the beaver was used for the expensive and fashionable hat called a beaver. (157)

Biggin close-fitting cap worn by babies and children. (139)

Billiment a decorative border often made of gold and studded with jewels that was used to edge the upper curve of a French hood and the lower (called nether) curve. Also worn separately as a hair ornament. (23) (67) (121)

Blackwork black silk embroidery on white linen. (36) (52) (108) (114) (137)

Bobbin lace a patterned lace made from threads attached to bobbins. (62) (79)

Bodyes a bodice was referred to as a 'pair of bodyes' (also spelt 'boddies') as it was made in two parts joined together at the side. (20)*

Bombast padding made from cotton, wool or horsehair that was used to produce a stiff, swollen shape.

Bongrace the projecting, usually detached brim of a bonnet, cap, or coif worn to protect the complexion. (118) (129) (137)* (153)

Bonnet a soft style of headwear with a brim and crown that was worn by men and women throughout the century. (8) (19) (31) (79)

Boothose over-stocking with richly embroidered top that would be turned down over the boot. (140)

Breastplate the section of armour that covered the breast. (114) (124) (155)

Breeches from about 1570 this term denoted an alternative style of legwear to trunk hose. It was worn with separate stockings and covered the area from the waist to the knee. See also *Venetians* and *galligaskins*. (96) (127) (132)

Brocade silk material woven with a pattern in gold, silver of contrasting colours. Patterns were usually floral or geometric and were sometimes raised. (37) (39) (107)

Canions Tubular extension of the hose which closely fitted the leg to below the kneecap. (102)* (148) (155)

Carcenet Heavy necklace made of gold and jewels that resembled a collar and was worn around the throat. (49) (85)

Caul hair net made of gold thread or silk, lined and decorated. (48) (59) (98)

Chemise another term for smock; a lady's linen undergarment. (24) (72) (74) (129)

Chin-clout large square of material worn over the chin, often seen in pictures of country women. (77) (82)

Chopines Italian shoes set on a high column of cork. (132)

Close-bodied gown gown that was shaped to the waist from where it fell in folds to the ground. (64)

Cloth of gold a material woven with a warp of pure gold threads and weft of silk; sometimes both could be gold. Used by royalty and the nobility.

Coat a general term for an upper garment. (25) (88)

Cod-piece bag-like appendage, attached by points to the hose, that concealed the opening in the front of the hose. (19) (45) (91)

Coif small linen cap which covered the head and was tied under the chin. (28) (65)

Colley-Westonward way of wearing a mandilion, with one sleeve hanging over the chest and one at the back. (117)

Copotain hat with a high conical crown, also called sugar-loaf because of its shape. (120) (130)

Cutwork lace of Italian origin made by cutting material into squares and then filling the spaces with geometric design. Also called *reticella* (108)

Damask rich silk made with either a floral or a geometric pattern. (43)

Doublet close-fitting garment worn over the shirt. (19) (47) (116) (151)

Dutch cloak a sleeved cloak, usually guarded. (110)

English hood also called the gable or pediment head-dress – consisted of a pointed arch which framed the face. There were variations in the structure of the hood during its fashionable lifespan from 1500 to c.1545. (2) (11) (15)

Ermine a fur only worn by the nobility and royalty. (51) (138) (143)

Falling band a shirt collar that has been turned down. (130) (133) (147)

Farthingale an understructure made with hoops which increased in circumference from the waist to the feet.

Forehead cloth triangular piece of material that was worn over a matching coif. (65)

Forepart triangular piece of material that filled in the central parted section of the skirt. (36) (56) (105)

French cloak long full cloak generally worn draped over the left shoulder (125) (147)

French farthingale a wheel-shaped structure worn under the skirt so that the skirt would be carried out at right angles before falling vertically to the feet. It was worn with a slight tilt forward, a tilt that became increasingly exaggerated after 1600. (128) (150)

French hood small hood worn far back on the head that consisted of curved front border and horseshoe-shaped curve on the top of the crown. (23) (32)

Fur stole usually made of sable and marten and lined with silk, its ends could be tipped with gold or a jewelled mount. It could be either placed around the neck or suspended by a chain from the girdle. (52) (137)*

Galligaskins full baggy breeches. (127)

Garters ornamented bands of silk or ribbon that secured stockings. (102)* (157)

Gauze transparent woven silk material. (80) (153)

Girdle narrow cord, band or chain that followed the waistline. It was usually decorated and, in the case of female dress, used to support a number of items. (34) (49) (150)

Gorget steel collar worn by the military. (92) (114)

Guards band of material either used as a decorative border or to cover a seam. It was made of a contrasting material and colour to the garment. (77) (123)

Hangers support for a sword that was attached to the sword-belt. (102)*

Hanging sleeve a false decorative sleeve that usually matched the doublet if worn by a man and the bodice if worn by a woman. (64) (115) (150)

Head-rail a square of starched linen arranged around the head; during the later part of the century it would be trimmed with lace and spangles and wired into elaborate shapes. (99) (126)

Hose the covering for a man's body from waist to feet. The term 'hose' was usually applied to the upper portion and did not denote stockings until the mid-seventeenth century. Stockings were referred to as nether stocks or nether stockings.

Jacket waist-length garment worn for warmth.

Jerkin sleeved or sleeveless fitted garment worn over the doublet. (69) (75) (130) (157)

Kerchief (also called neckerchief) a large white square of material, folded lengthways and used as a shawl for the shoulders. (61) (77)

Kersey light-weight narrow wool cloth.

Kirtle before 1545 this term denoted bodice and skirt but after that date the skirt alone. (1) (5) (32)

Lappet the decorated border of an English hood that was extended so that it hung down on either side of the face. After 1525 these lappets were turned up at ear level and pinned to the crown. (11) (14) (38)

Lawn (see *linen*)

Linen a material woven from flax that ranged in quality from coarse buckram and dowlas to lawn, a very fine and expensive linen used for ruffs, collars and rails.

Loose gown an over-garment that fell in loose folds from the shoulders. Also called an open gown. (72) (52)

Love lock long curled lock of hair arranged to fall over the shoulder. (133)

Mandilion loose jacket with a standing collar and hanging sleeves. (117)

Mantle if worn on ceremonial occasions it was a long garment that was open in front and reached to the ground. Also called a veil in inventories and appears to have been worn like a shawl. When mentioned in this context it was usually made from a diaphanous material.

Marquisetto a beard that was cut close to the chin. (110) (114)

Mary Stuart hood lawn hood wired into a heart shape. (99) (105)

Mask worn outdoors and in bed to protect the complexion. Also worn at masques to disguise the features. (141)

Milan bonnet a style of headwear that was popular during the first four decades of the century. It had a soft, pleated crown and a broad brim that was turned up and slit on either side. (6)

Milliner one that sold fancy goods and fashionable accessories.

Muckminder slang term for handkerchief or napkin.

Mules flat, backless shoes. (60)

Nightcap linen cap, usually embroidered, worn indoors by men.

Nightgown loose, lined gown worn by men and women either indoors for warmth and comfort or outdoors as an overgarment. Usually lined with fur. (103)

Panes method of decorating material either by slashing the whole length vertically, leaving top and bottom joined, or by applying separate strips of material that are joined top and bottom. (70) (86) (102)*

Pantofles overshoes with long front uppers and thick cork soles. (112)

Partlet decorative accessory that covered the upper part of the chest. (11) (67) (74)* (98)

Pauldrons section of armour that covered the shoulders. (114)

Peascod name given to exaggerated style of doublet fashionable in the 1580s and 1590s. (116) (131) (151)

Petticoat underskirt. (77)

Pinking small holes or slits cut into material and arranged to form a pattern. (62) (91) (92)

Pickadil either stiffened tabs set at right-angles to form a border or, at the end of the century, a wired or stiffened support for a standing band. (83) (86)

Pickdevant short, pointed beard usually worn with a brushed-up moustache. (119) (122)

Plackard a separate ornamental accessory that covered the chest. (21)

Points ties with metal tags. (90) (93)*

Pomander a perforated container for perfume. (57) (67)

Puffs decorative effect produced when material was drawn out through slashes and panes. (19) (74)* (85)

Rail square of material folded horizontally and worn on the head or round the shoulders like a shawl.

Rebato shaped collar pinned to the bodice and wired so that it stands up round the back of the head. (125)

Rerebrace section of armour that covers the area above the elbow. (114)

Ruching material that has been gathered together in close folds so that it can be used as a trimming. (126) (154)

Ruffs originally the frill that edged the standing collar of a shirt. Ruffs increased in size until, by the 1570s, they had become separate articles. Through the use of starch and setting-sticks ruffs could be very wide and consist of many layers. (67) (84) (139) (152)

Russet coarse woollen homespun material largely used by country people. (96)

Sable fur worn by the nobility and the wealthy. (18) (119)*

Shag thick-piled cloth often used for linings. (147)

Slashing slits of varying length cut in a garment and arranged in a pattern. (69) (83)

Snoskyn a muff – a fashionable accessory for women at the end of the century. (125)

Spanish cloak a full, short cloak with a hood. (112)

Spanish farthingale understructure which produced either a funnel-shaped or bell-shaped skirt. (39) (49) (107)

Startups loose leather shoes worn by country workers. (96)

Stockings were worn by men and women. They could be tailored, or knitted, and be made from a wide range of materials, silk being the most expensive. (116)

Stomacher inverted triangle of stiffened material that was attached to the front of the bodice. (149) (150)

Tippet short shoulder cape worn with a gown. (3)

Trunk hose a style of hose which swelled out from the waistband to turn directly onto the thighs. (92) (102)* (116)

Trunk sleeve a sleeve with a very wide top part that narrowed to a closed wrist, its swollen shape achieved by means of padding. (107) (150)

Underpropper wire frame attached to the collar which supports the ruff pinned to it. This enabled the wearer to tilt his ruff at the required angle. (102)

Valance border of drapery that was hung round the canopy of a bed. (125)

Vambrace section of armour that covers the area between the elbow and the gauntlet. (114)

Velvet a very popular material among the upper classes that was available in a wide range of colours which could be either plain or figured. Figured velvet was woven in two colours with two and sometimes three piles.

Venetians full breeches closed at the knee. They could be a. voluminous throughout (93)*. b. close-fitting (130) and c. pear-shaped (83).

Waistcoat informal jacket-style garment worn by men and women. (143)

Wing roll of stiffened material that hid the join between sleeve and armhole. It could be decorated in a variety of ways. (74)* (86) (98) (145)